Discover Florida's Amazing Birding and Wildlife Trails

Yeliz N. Nascimento

<u>***Funny helpful tips:***</u>

Stay persistent; perseverance often differentiates dreams achieved from those abandoned.

Your essence is a light; let it shine brightly, guiding and uplifting others.

*Discover Florida's Amazing Birding and Wildlife Trails :
Uncover Florida's Enthralling Wildlife Sanctuaries and
Birdwatching Destinations for Nature Enthusiasts.*

Life advices:

Stay proactive in risk management; anticipating challenges ensures better preparedness.

In the meadow of dreams, chase your aspirations with unwavering belief.

Introduction

This is a comprehensive resource for birding and wildlife enthusiasts in Florida. It provides information on various clusters and locations across the state that offer excellent opportunities for observing birds and other wildlife species.

The guide starts by introducing the Perdido Cluster, which is an area known for its diverse bird species. It then proceeds to highlight other clusters such as the Migrant's Rest Cluster, Blackwater Cluster, Choctawhatchee Cluster, Dogwood Cluster, Kentucky Warbler Cluster, Indigo Bunting Cluster, Cape Cluster, Pitcher Plant & Peregrine Cluster, Bluffs Cluster, Talquin Cluster, White-breasted Nuthatch Cluster, and Mississippi Kite Cluster. Each cluster offers unique habitats and species to explore.

The guide also emphasizes the importance of birding and wildlife viewing ethics, providing guidelines for responsible and respectful behavior while observing birds and wildlife. It encourages visitors to consider factors such as minimizing disturbances, respecting private property, and following regulations and guidelines set by land managers.

Additionally, the guide provides information on resources for birding and wildlife viewing, including websites, books, and other reference materials that can enhance the experience. It also offers suggestions for obtaining more information about specific locations and clusters.

The guide addresses the economic impact of birding and wildlife tourism, encouraging visitors to support local economies and conservation efforts through their activities. It emphasizes the importance of sustainable tourism practices and the positive contributions that birders and wildlife viewers can make to the preservation of natural habitats and species.

Lastly, the guide acknowledges the coexistence of birding and wildlife viewing with hunting activities on public lands. It emphasizes the need for sharing public lands and respecting the rights and safety of all outdoor enthusiasts.

This is a valuable resource for anyone interested in exploring Florida's diverse bird species and wildlife habitats. It provides essential information, ethical guidelines, and resources to enhance the birding and wildlife viewing experience while promoting conservation and responsible outdoor recreation.

Contents

Map A
Perdido
Cluster

1   Big Lagoon State Park   *Gateway**

County: Escambia
Nearest city: Pensacola
Physical address: 12301 Gulf Beach Hwy., Pensacola, 32507
Coordinates: 30.321628° N, -87.403734° W
Gazetteer page: 42
Size: 732 acres

An ideal gateway for the Birding and Wildlife Trail! This site nicely represents the diversity of Panhandle habitats, all in the boundaries of a single park. The bayfront offers sandy expanses for wintering Black-bellied Plovers, Dunlin and Least Sandpipers, and winter ducks like Lesser Scaup, Redhead, Buflehead and Red-breasted Mergansers can be seen diving in the bay from the East Beach tower. Common Loons call on foggy mornings in early spring (an uncommon occurrence in peninsular Florida), and a diversity of gulls and terns feed in area waters. Migrants like Yellow-billed Cuckoos arriving off the Gulf make landfall in the spring and feed on insects in hammocks in the campground and along the Yaupon and Long Pond Trails. Long Pond Trail skirts some freshwater wetlands, then stretches into the Cookie Trail leading along the north edge of the lagoon onto a scrubby point, peppered with pines favored by Yellow-bellied Sapsuckers, Northern Flickers and Brown-headed Nuthatches. Check with staff for information on birding and wildlife events going on in the Panhandle; binoculars are also available for loan from the ranger station.

Directions: Due west of Pensacola, drive south on SR 173/Blue Angel Pkwy. and turn right (west) on SR 292/Sorrento Rd. After 2.7 mi., turn left (south) on CR 293/Bauer Rd; the entrance to the park is at the end of CR 293.

Open year round, 8 AM to sundown. (850) 492-1595
www.floridastateparks.org/biglagoon

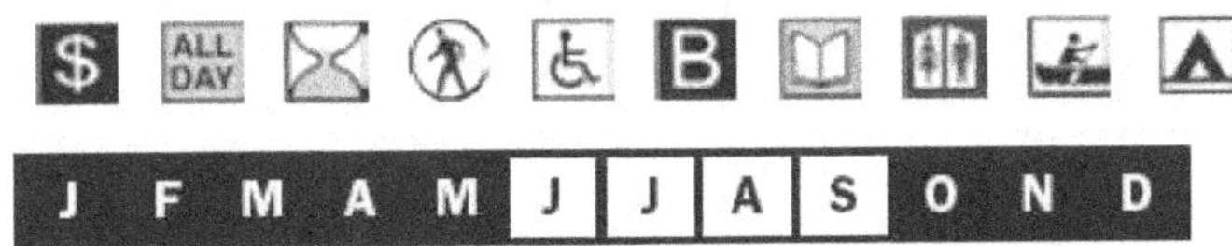

*see "Gateways" section for more information.

2 Gulf Islands National Seashore: Perdido Key Area

County: Escambia

Nearest city: Pensacola

Physical address: Johnson Beach Rd., Pensacola, 32507

Coordinates: 30.298946° N, -87.417659° W

Gazetteer page: 42

Size: 1,041 acres

This property encompasses the eastern tip of Perdido Key at the mouth of Pensacola Bay, with miles of undeveloped beach. To begin, turn left (north) 0.25 mile past the fee booth and park at the end of the road. A 0.5-mile loop with a boardwalk nature trail begins here, which can be good in spring for Neotropical songbirds such as Swainson's Thrushes. Pine Warblers and Eastern Towhees call from the pinewoods while the boardwalk winds through marsh good for Clapper Rails and Spotted Sandpipers at muddy edges. Return to the main park road, which runs eastward for another 2 miles. Beach (south side) and lagoon (north side) accesses along the road allow looks at Northern Gannets October through March, and a diversity of gulls, terns and various shorebirds year-round. Least Terns and Snowy Plovers nest in the protected areas on the north side of the road and elsewhere, so be careful not to disturb them. Small coves on Big Lagoon shelter ducks and Common Loons from the winter wind, offering good, close views. Extended hours are available (ask about Night Owl permits), and primitive camping is allowed (with permit) on the east end of the key.

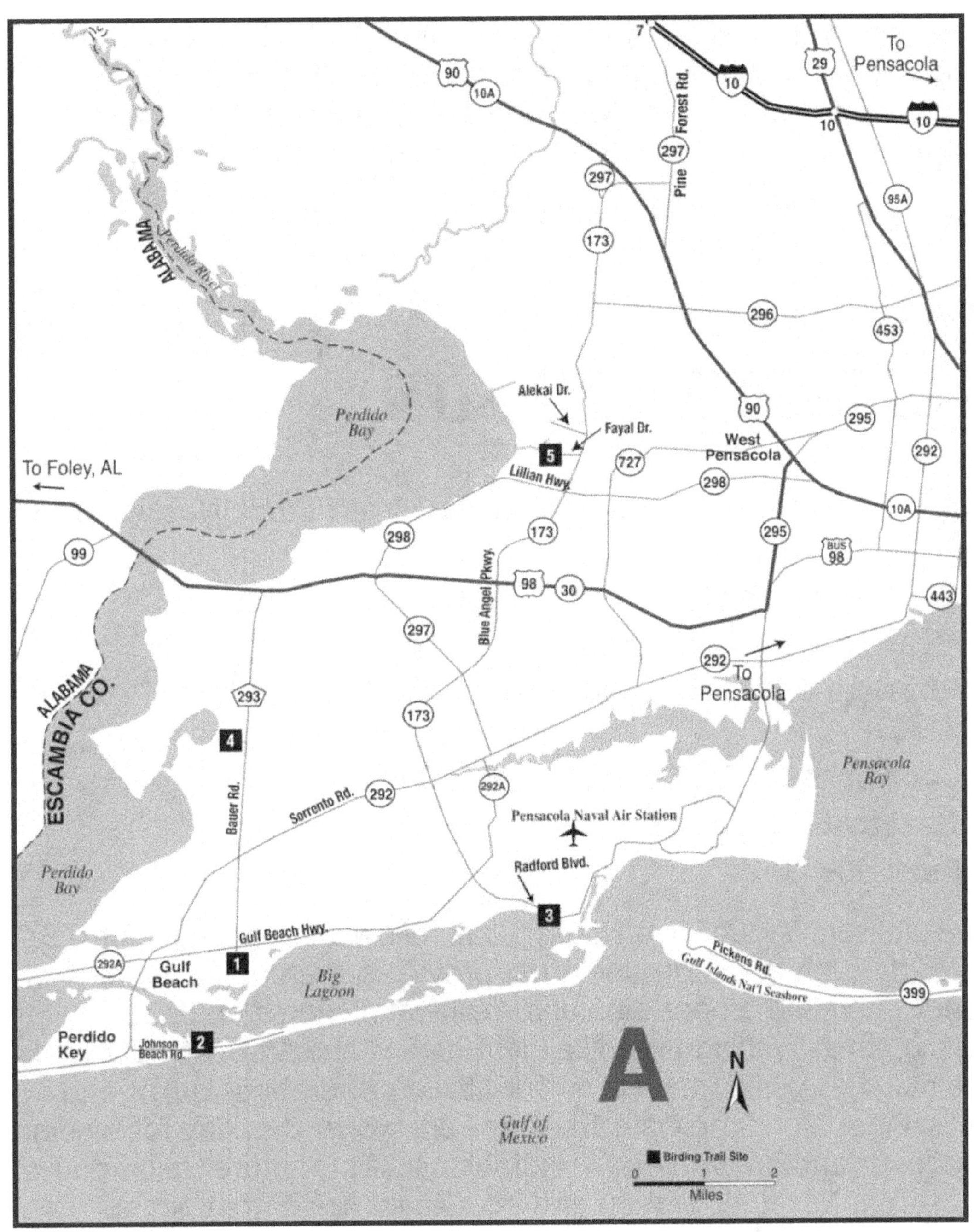

To Pensacola
90
10A
7
10
29
10
10
297
Pine Forest Rd.
297
95A
173
296
453
Alekai Dr.
Perdido Bay
Fayal Dr.
5
West Pensacola
295
292
To Foley, AL
727
Lillian Hwy.
298
298
173
10A
99
173
295
BUS 98
98
30
Blue Angel Pkwy.
443
297
292
To Pensacola
ALABAMA
ESCAMBIA CO.
293
173
4
292A
Bauer Rd.
Sorrento Rd.
292
Pensacola Naval Air Station
Pensacola Bay
Perdido Bay
Radford Blvd.
3
Gulf Beach Hwy.
292A
Gulf Beach
1
Big Lagoon
Pickens Rd.
Gulf Islands Nat'l Seashore
399
Perdido Key
Johnson Beach Rd.
2
A
N
Gulf of Mexico
Birding Trail Site
0   1   2
Miles
ALABAMA
Perdido River

Directions: Due west of Pensacola, drive south on SR 173/Blue Angel Pkwy. and turn right (west) on SR 292/Sorrento Rd. After approx. 6.5 mi., turn left (east) on Johnson Beach Rd.; the entrance/pay station is 0.5 mi. ahead past Johnson Beach.

Open year round, 7 AM to sunset. (850) 934-2600
www.nps.gov/guis

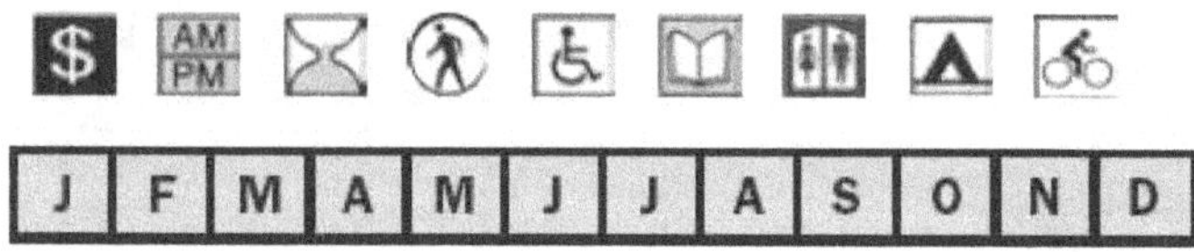

3   Naval Air Station Pensacola: Trout Point Nature Trail

County: Escambia

Nearest city: Pensacola

Physical address: S. Blue Angel Pkwy./Radford Blvd., Pensacola, 32507

Coordinates: 30.333322° N, -87.338438° W

Gazetteer page: 42

Size: 40+ acres

The pleasant Trout Point Nature Trail follows a boardwalk for 0.5 miles through the interdune area, providing the unique vantage of sandy shoreline on one side and freshwater marsh and open water on the other. Wading birds like night-herons and Snowy Egrets work the marshes while the beachfront attracts shorebirds, terns and gulls. Pines along the waterfront trail are worth checking for feeding songbirds and Brown-headed Nuthatches. This nature trail is part of Pensacola Naval Air Station and occasional noise from aircraft should be expected. At the entrance security gate, tell the security offcer you are visiting Trout Point Nature Trail. Heightened security levels may limit access, so call ahead for information.

Directions: Due west of Pensacola, drive south on SR 173/Blue Angel Pkwy. to the west gate of Pensacola Naval Air Station. Continue straight through the gate on Radford Blvd. Turn right at the trail entrance (0.5 mi. from security gate). Continue on the unpaved road for 0.25 mi. to the trailhead and parking.

Open 6 AM to 30 min. before sunset. (850) 452-3100
www.dodpif.org/checklists/napf.htm

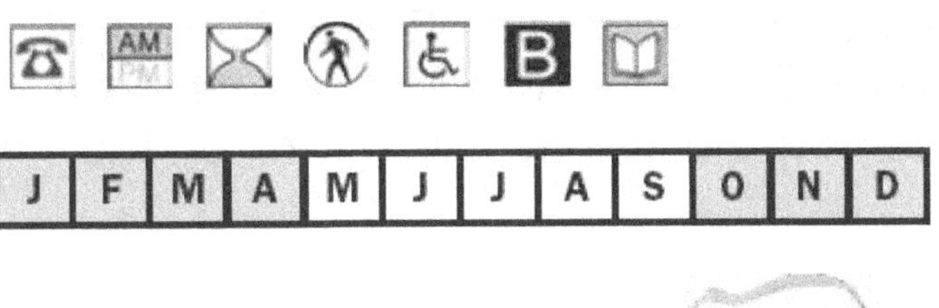

4 Tarkiln Bayou Preserve State Park

County: Escambia

Nearest city: Pensacola

Physical address: CR 293/Bauer Rd., Pensacola, 32506

Coordinates: 30.372923° N, -87.402335° W

Gazetteer page: 42

Size: 4,197 acres

From the parking lot, hike the trail west through flatwoods, listening for the "squeaky toy" call of Brown-headed Nuthatches, the wavering trills of Pine Warblers and the harsh, squawking sounds of Yellow-breasted Chats. For a shorter hike, veer left at the fork. The paved trail leads to a boardwalk through a titi forest (listen for breeding White-eyed Vireos), which emerges on the sheltered bayou. Scan the reeds for rails and waders. For a longer hike, veer right at the fork, following the trail along the bayou's far side, past a rare pitcher plant bog, to the end on Perdido Bay. Across the street from the parking lot, upland sandhill habitats host Common Ground-Doves year-round, and Common Nighthawks on late spring/summer evenings. Bring water year-round and expect mosquitoes in warmer months.

Directions: West of Pensacola, drive south on SR 173/Blue Angel Pkwy. and turn right (west) on 292/Sorrento Rd. After 2.7 mi., turn right (north) on CR 293/Bauer Rd; the entrance is 2.2 mi. on the left.

Open year round, 8 AM to sundown. (850) 492-1595
www.floridastateparks.org/tarkilnbayou

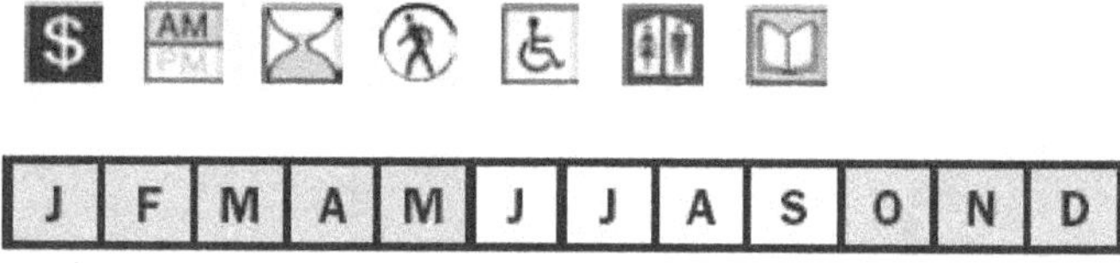

| J | F | M | A | M | J | J | A | S | O | N | D |

5 ECUA Bayou Marcus Wetlands

County: Escambia

Nearest city: Bellview/Pensacola

Physical address: 3050 Fayal Dr., Pensacola, 32526 (main)
Alekai Dr., Pensacola, 32526 (Alekai Dr. entrance)

Coordinates: 30.436991° N, -87.325980° W (main entrance)
30.444484° N, -87.332614° W (Alekai Dr. entrance)

Gazetteer page: 42

Size: 1,100 acres

From the parking lot, this functioning wastewater treatment facility has nearly 8,000 feet of boardwalk through the titi-lined wetlands created by the plant's treated wastewater discharge. As you enter the boardwalk, the frst large pond on the left hosts wintering Blue-winged Teal, Hooded Merganser, Buflehead and Common Goldeneye to name a few. Swamp, Song and White-throated Sparrows exploit the weedy edges and Brown-headed Nuthatches and Pine Warblers call from the adjacent pinewoods. The odd Groove-billed Ani sighting keeps interest in this site high. Please be considerate, as this is a fully functional utilities plant; birder access is at the management's discretion. Recent site improvements include four shade stops on the boardwalk, trail surface improvements, publication racks, bird checklist and interpretive signs.

Directions: From the intersection of SR 173/Blue Angel Pkwy. and CR 298/Lillian Hwy., go north on Blue Angel Pkwy. for 1.1 mi. to the ECUA sign at Fayal Dr. Turn left (west) and drive to the entrance gate. Park and enter through the fence to access the boardwalk. A second entrance on Alekai Dr. (formerly Ramsey Beach Rd.) is now handicapped accessible. To access this entrance, go back to Blue Angel Pkwy. and turn left (north). After 0.3 mi., turn left (west) onto Alekai Dr. and go 0.4 mi.

Open daily, 7 AM to 6 PM. (850) 458-1658, (850) 476-0480
www.ecua.l.gov/green/bayou-marcus-nature-trail-walk

J	F	M	A	M	J	J	A	S	O	N	D

Map B

Migrant's Rest Cluster

6 University of West Florida: Edward Ball Nature Trail

County: Escambia
Nearest city: Pensacola
Physical address: 11000 University Pkwy., Pensacola, 32514
Coordinates: 30.550723° N, -87.221716° W
Gazetteer page: 26
Size: 15 acres

The Edward Ball Nature Trail includes a short boardwalk through a nice ravine and swamp, with Prothonotary Warbler-laden cypress trees above and wading egrets below. Songbirds like Northern Parulas, Summer Tanagers and Great Crested Flycatchers frequent the area, and migration in spring and fall can yield some interesting visiting species. Swallow-tailed Kites may be seen overhead in spring and summer. The slope is steep and the boardwalk shows its age, so don't get so distracted by the birds that you forget to watch your step!

Directions: From US 90A/Nine Mile Rd. north of Pensacola, turn north on University Pkwy. At the end of University Pkwy., turn left (west) onto Campus Dr. Take the 4th left, then another immediate left into Parking Lot G. Park and walk behind the Science Building

(Bldg. 13) to the trail entrance. Campus maps and MANDATORY PARKING PASSES can be obtained at the Information Center (1st right after turning onto Campus Dr.).

Open daily, dawn to dusk. (850) 474-2580
www.uwf.edu

7 Wayside Park and Pensacola Visitor Information Center

County: Escambia
Nearest city: Pensacola
Physical address: 1401 E. Gregory St., Pensacola, 32502
Coordinates: 30.417865° N, -87.193398° W
Gazetteer page: 42
Size: 9 acres

Worth a quick stop to view gulls and terns; the waterfront, fishing bridge and offshore breakwater all host a variety of ages of Herring, Ring-billed and Laughing Gulls, Forster's and Royal Terns and more. Common Loons feed very close to shore, and sport nearly complete breeding plumage in February/March before they return north. Bring your spotting scope to check the bay for wintering ducks and Horned Grebes.

Directions: From I-10 north of Pensacola, take exit 12 for I-110 and head south. Take exit 1B for Chase St. and head east. Continue east on Chase St. until it ends at US 98/Bayfront Pkwy. and take a left (east). Drive approx. 0.3 mi. and turn left (northeast) on N. 17th Ave.

After 300 ft., turn right (southeast) on E. Gregory St. Parking is 350 ft. ahead.

Open 24 hrs/day. (800) 874-1234
www.visitpensacola.com

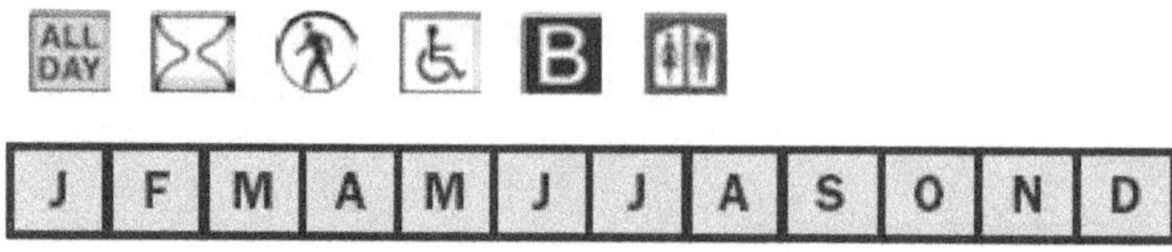

8 Project GreenShores

County: Escambia

Nearest city: Pensacola

Physical address: Bayfront Pkwy., Pensacola, 32502

Coordinates: 30.417634° N, -87.194486° W

Gazetteer page: 42

Size: 15 acres

Project GreenShores is a restoration project undertaken by a suite of advocates and agencies. Located across from the Pensacola Visitor Center along Bayfront Pkwy., the project is systematically establishing an emergent marsh and oyster reef along the waterfront. The area has historically been good for birds like Osprey, Brown Pelican and Royal Tern, but as the salt marsh grasses take root, the birds are responding! Yellow-crowned Night-Heron, Semipalmated Plover, Black-necked Stilt and more ply the fats and shoreline. Park and walk the waterfront to the west along the bay shore; restoration efforts continue past the Missing Children's Memorial on Hawkshaw Lagoon (across from Veterans Park) to Bartram Park. Look for Loggerhead Shrike on the far southern end of the property just before the bridge.

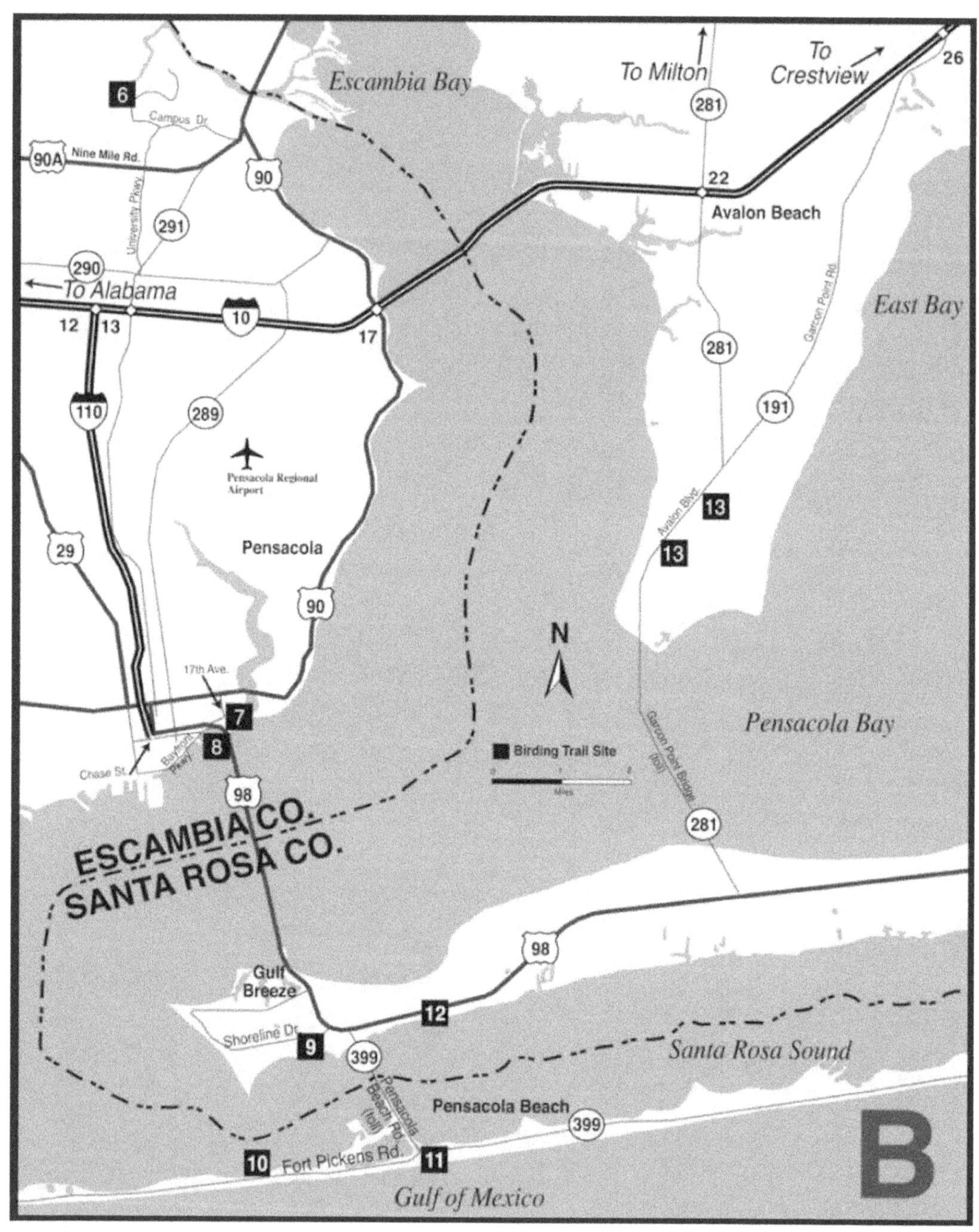

Directions: From I-10 north of Pensacola, take exit 12 for I-110 and head south. Take exit 1B for Chase St. and head east. Continue east

on Chase St. until it ends at US 98/Bayfront Pkwy. and turn left
(east). The site and parking are approx. 0.3 mi. on the right, 100 ft.
past the intersection with N. 17th Ave. and 0.25 mi. before the
Pensacola Bay Bridge.

Open daily, dawn to dusk. (850) 595-8300
www.dep.state.f.us/northwest/Ecosys/section/greenshores.htm

9 Shoreline Park South

County: Santa Rosa
Nearest city: Gulf Breeze
Physical address: 800 Shoreline Dr., Gulf Breeze, 32561
Coordinates: 30.354244° N, -87.177670° W
Gazetteer page: 42
Size: 100 acres

Shoreline Park South is a small sound-side park in Gulf Breeze,
which lies between Fort Pickens and the mainland as the bird fies.
This ensures it's on the direct path of migrants coming in off the Gulf
in spring. In winter, bird the waterfront for grebes and loons
(occasional Pacific and Red-throated in years when vagrant birds are
prevalent). Wintering ducks like Lesser Scaup, Buffehead and even
occasional Common Goldeneye can be viewed from the pier. Nearer
the entrance, bird the loop trails through oak hammock excellent for
resident Pine Warblers, Carolina Chickadees and Pileated
Woodpeckers, as well as migrant Black-throated Blue and Worm-
eating Warblers, Swainson's Thrushes, Orchard Orioles and more.

This site is busy on warm weather weekends. Recent amenities include a boardwalk nature trail, waterfront boardwalk, picnic shelters and restrooms. Many park features are handicapped accessible. A viewing deck with seats provides good elevation for scoping winter waterbirds.

Directions: From US 98 in Gulf Breeze, turn west on Shoreline Dr. (just west of Pensacola Beach Rd./toll bridge). Go 0.1 mi. to the first intersection, and turn left (southwest) to stay on Shoreline Dr. The entrance is located 0.7 mi. on the left (south) side of the road.

Open 24 hours/day. (850) 934-5140
www.gulfbreezerecreationcenter.com

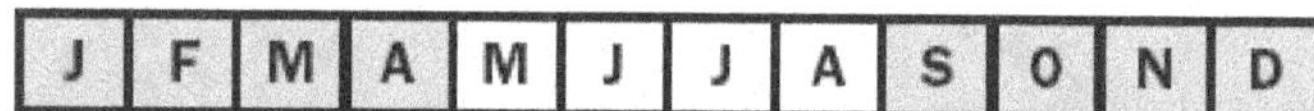

10   Gulf Islands National Seashore: Fort Pickens Area

County: Escambia

Nearest city: Pensacola Beach

Physical address: 1400 Fort Pickens Rd., Pensacola Beach, 32561

Coordinates: 30.325672° N, -87.181354° W

Gazetteer page: 42

Size: 1,742 acres

This migratory hotspot is not to be missed in spring, as tired migrants make landfall after long overwater fights. Batteries Langdon and Worth are both good stops for migrants; closely check fowering oaks. Please respect closed areas protecting nesting birds: the beach here is prime for breeding Snowy Plovers and Least Terns spring through fall. Black Terns are ubiquitous in summer and early fall. By far, the fort and surrounding trails offer this site's most exciting birding. In open areas surrounding the fortifications, watch for sentinel fycatchers on any minor promontory. Gray Kingbirds breed here and Scissor-tailed Flycatchers are occasional in winter. The trails on the fort's bayside can be extraordinary for migrant songbirds like Tennessee, Cape May, and Magnolia Warblers and more. Morning is not necessarily the best time to see these birds; long-term sighting logs from dedicated local birders indicate these migrants can make landfall in early afternoon. Fallouts are exaggerated by early afternoon rain showers that ground migrants as soon as they reach land. Migrating raptors cruise the duneline in October and April. Loaner optics and field guides are available. Fort Pickens Road is prone to storm-related closures; check road condition at website below prior to departure.

Directions: From Pensacola, take US 98 east approx. 4.5 mi. to the south side of Gulf Breeze. Take SR 399/Pensacola Beach Rd. (toll bridge) south across Santa Rosa Sound to Pensacola Beach. Turn right (southwest) at Fort Pickens Rd. and head west for 2.5 mi. to the entrance.

Fort Pickens Area open 7 AM to 10 PM. (850) 934-2600
Historic Fort Pickens open 8 AM to sunset.
www.nps.gov/guis

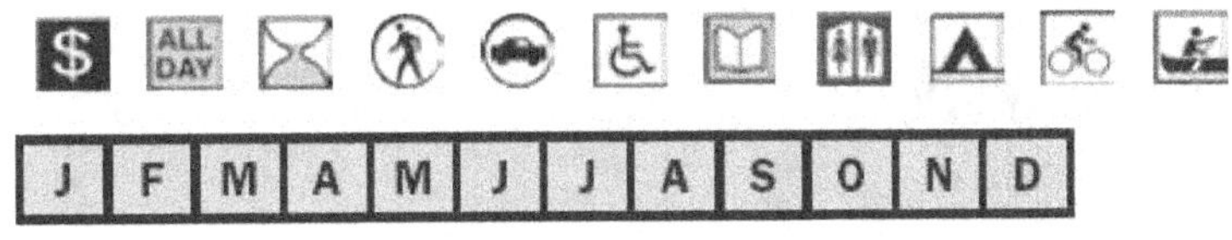

11 Pensacola Beach Gulf Pier

County: Escambia
Nearest city: Pensacola Beach
Physical address: 41 Fort Pickens Rd., Pensacola Beach, 32561
Coordinates: 30.332175° N, -87.142344° W
Gazetteer page: 43
Size: 0.25 miles

With binoculars alone, this site offers a fare of gulls and terns comparable to other area beach sites. However, with a spotting scope and a little blustery weather, this 0.25-mile pier can be a seawatcher's dream, offering a stable site away from the beach to scan out over the sea. More common sightings are wintering Common Loons and plunging gannets October through March. However, in periods of stormy weather in the Gulf of Mexico, tantalizing seabirds like Bridled and Sooty Terns and Sooty Shearwaters have been spotted from this location. Respect severe weather, but certainly don't let a little rain discourage you! This site is primarily a fishing pier, but welcomes birders too.

Directions: From Pensacola, take US 98/SR 30/Gulf Breeze Pkwy. south across the Pensacola Bay Bridge to the south side of Gulf Breeze. Take SR 399/Pensacola Beach Rd. (toll bridge) south across Santa Rosa Sound to Pensacola Beach. Turn right (southwest) at Fort Pickens Rd. and go 0.1 mi. to the first entrance on the left (south) side of the road (look for a large parking lot with a "beach ball" water tower).

Open 24 hours/day. (850) 934-7200
www.fishpensacolabeachpier.com

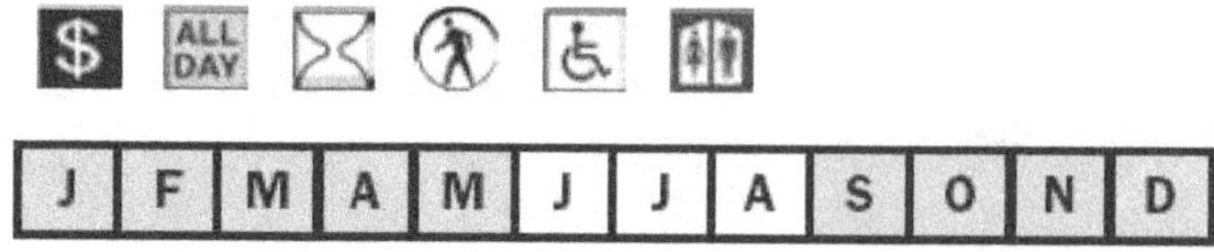

12   Gulf Islands National Seashore: Naval Live Oaks Area

County: Santa Rosa
Nearest city: Gulf Breeze
Physical address: 1801 Gulf Breeze Pkwy., Gulf Breeze, 32563
Coordinates: 30.364997° N, -87.131275° W
Gazetteer page: 42 and 43
Size: Size: 1,378 acres

This visitor center and park HQ for the national seashore spans the spit of land separating Santa Rosa Sound to the south from Pensacola Bay to the north. From the sound-side shoreline south of the visitor center parking, scope for Common Goldeneye, Lesser Scaup and other wintering ducks. As always in migration, check the live oaks for which this area was named; Black-and-white Warblers pick through resurrection fern on the sides of oaks in winter, and Brown Creepers are occasionally found scaling the trees.

Directions: From Pensacola, take US 98/SR 30/Gulf Breeze Pkwy. south across the Pensacola Bay Bridge to Gulf Breeze. Stay on US 98 East past the intersection with SR 399; the visitor center and headquarters are 1.8 mi. ahead on the right (south) side of the road.

Open 8 AM to sunset. (850) 934-2600
www.nps.gov/guis

13   Garcon Point Water Management Area: Garcon Point Trail

County: Santa Rosa

Nearest city: Milton/Gulf Breeze

Physical address: SR 281/CR 191, Milton, 32583

Coordinates: 30.470726° N, -87.084151° W (north entrance)
30.459271° N, -87.092904° W (south entrance)

Gazetteer page: 43

Size: 3,235 acres

Gorgeous wet prairie occupies much of this preserve, with slightly elevated patches of longleaf pine-wiregrass community breaking the otherwise unobstructed horizon. A habitat of extremes, this landscape burns frequently and absorbs lots of rainfall; trails may occasionally hold water so immersible shoes are recommended. Biting fies and ticks are quite unpleasant from April to October, but the sheer beauty of this site makes it a must-see from November to March. Wet prairie sparrows like Henslow's and Le Conte's occasionally winter here and Cooper's Hawks cruise the prairie for prey like Eastern Towhees and Loggerhead Shrikes. Yellow Rails have been found here in winter. Pine Warblers call from the tree line and rare pitcher plants crowd the trail (stay on the trail to protect these Panhandle specialties!). From the south entrance, access the 1.7-mile loop trail through scrubby oaks and past an ephemeral wetland. From the north trailhead, the North Spur Trail runs 1.2 miles south to join the loop trail on its north border. See the Florida Trail Association's website for additional information. Access to and from Pensacola Beach via SR 821 requires toll and may result in delays during peak travel times.

Directions: From I-10 south of Milton, take exit 22 for SR 281/Avalon Blvd. and head south. After 4 mi., this road will merge with CR 191/Garcon Point Rd. Drive approx. 0.7 mi. past the intersection with CR 191; the north trailhead is on the left (east) side of the road. The south trailhead is 1 mi. farther, also on the left (east) side of the road. If coming from the south on SR 281, the southern entrance is located 0.25 mi. north of the bridge's toll booth.

Open dawn to dusk. (850) 484-5125, (850) 539-5999
www.nwfwater.com/lands/recreation/area/garcon-point/
www.foridatrail.org

J	F	M	A	M	J	J	A	S	O	N	D

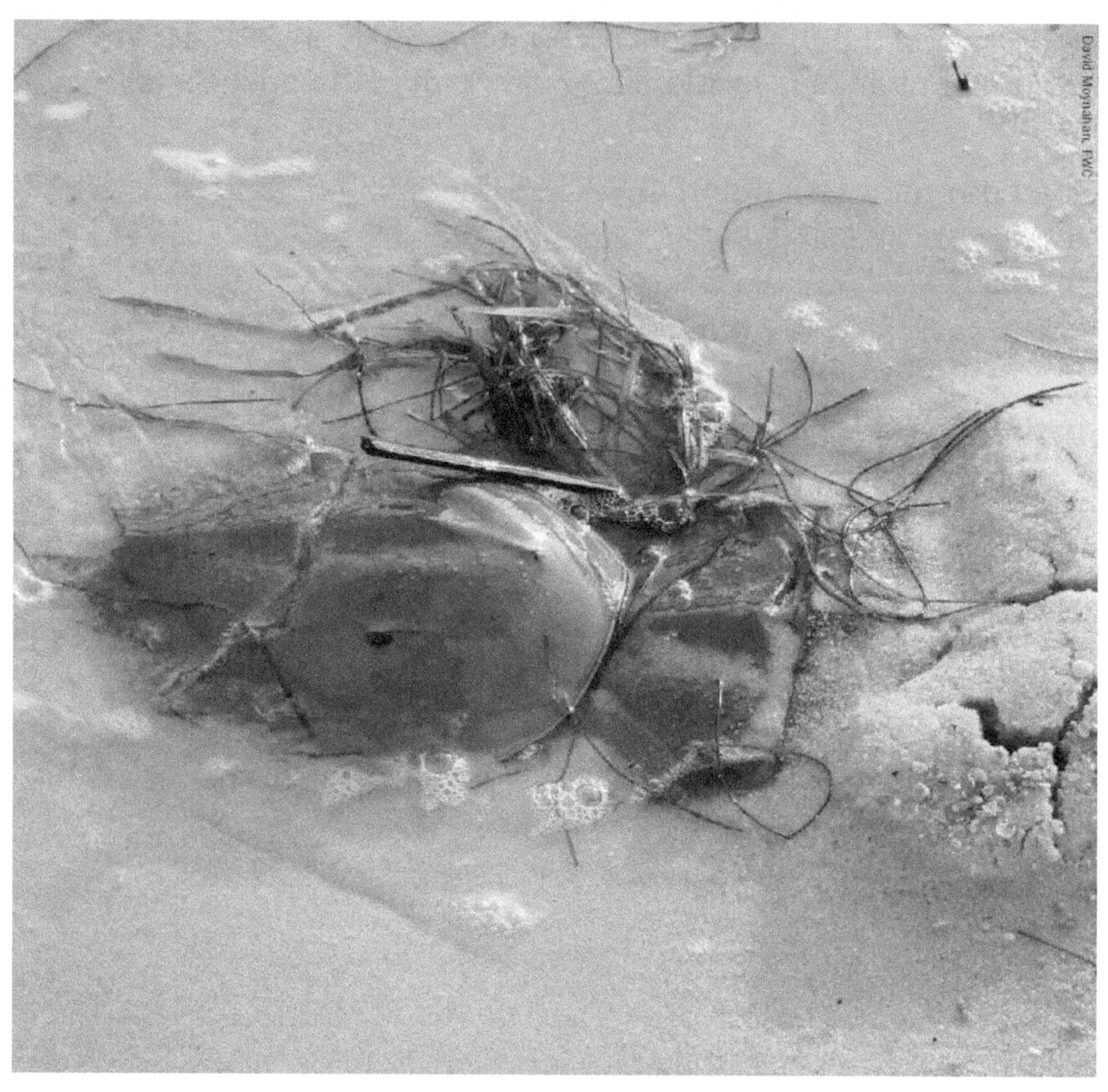

Horseshoe Crabs

Map C
Blackwater Cluster

14   Blackwater River State Forest: Hutton Unit

County: Santa Rosa
Nearest city: Holt
Physical address: Deaton Bridge Rd., Milton, 32583
Coordinates: 30.685874° N, -86.876366° W
Gazetteer page: 27
Size: 7,629 acres

This site adjacent to Blackwater River State Park is worth a quick stop to listen for Bachman's Sparrow in spring and summer – if they are singing you'll likely hear them from the parking lot! The available habitat is turkey oak/pine uplands common throughout the Panhandle, and not as productive for birding as other habitats may be. Still, in springtime, a quick peek can never hurt. Less than 1 mile from the entrance on H9 Road (across from Boundary Line Rd.) you should encounter species such as Red-headed Woodpecker, Brown-headed Nuthatch, Eastern Bluebird and Great Crested Flycatcher. Gates are open to general vehicular traffic from May 1 to October 1; gates will be closed in hunting season (hunters check in through a different gate). If the gate on Deaton Bridge Rd. is locked, you may use the parking lot next to the gate and walk in. Additional entrances are located at Pond Road off US 90 and at the intersection of Deaton Bridge Rd. and Indian Ford Rd. Take care driving on area clay roads –

they can be slippery when wet. The Florida National Scenic Trail winds through the site and is open to hikers year round. A WMA map is available from the FWC website. Seasonal hunting takes place at this GFBWT site; please see Sharing Florida's public lands during hunting season for information on dates, regulations and more.

Directions: From Milton, take US 90 east for approx. 9.5 mi. to Harold. Turn left (north) on Deaton Bridge Rd. and drive 1.8 mi.; the entrance and parking area are on the left (west) side of the road, directly across from Boundary Line Rd. From I-10 eastbound, take exit 31 for SR 87 and head north to US 90. Turn right (east) on US 90 and follow it for 5.8 mi. to Deaton Bridge Rd. From I-10 westbound, take exit 45 for Log Lake Rd. and go north to US 90. Turn left (west) and follow US 90 for 8.7 mi. to Deaton Bridge Rd.

Open dawn to dusk. (850) 957-6140
MyFWC.com/viewing/recreation/wmas/cooperative/blackwater
www.freshfromforida.com/Divisions-Ofices/Florida-Forest-Service

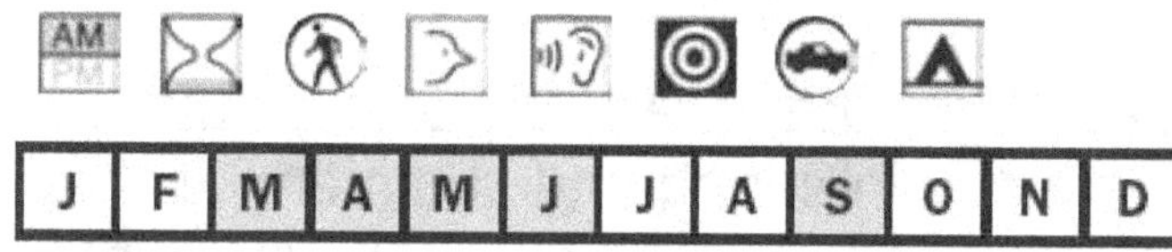

15 Blackwater River State Park

County: Santa Rosa
Nearest city: Holt
Physical address: 7720 Deaton Bridge Rd., Holt, 32564
Coordinates: 30.711943° N, -86.879987° W
Gazetteer page: 27
Size: 635 acres

This site is a popular swimming, canoeing and picnicking area in warm weather, but offers nice access to foodplain hiking trails good for Yellow-billed Cuckoos and Hairy Woodpeckers in late spring and summer. Broad-winged, Red-tailed and Red-shouldered Hawks are common and Wood Thrushes and Prothonotary Warblers breed here. Brown-headed Nuthatches squeak from pines in the uplands; these delightful acrobats are a joy to watch. The brief campground trail and the 0.9-mile Chain of Lakes Nature Trail are best for birding. The trails can be wet at times of high water, so wear shoes you don't mind getting muddy! Loaner optics and ield guides are available.

Directions: From Milton, take US 90 east for approx. 9.5 mi. to Harold. Turn left (north) on Deaton Bridge Rd. and drive 3.9 mi.; the entrance is on the right (east) side. Additional parking areas (fee required) are located at either end of the bridge. Access the Chain of Lakes Nature Trail at the south end of the bridge. From I-10 eastbound, take exit 31 for SR 87 and head north to US 90/SR 10. Turn right (east) on US 90 and follow it for 5.8 mi. to Deaton Bridge Rd. From I-10 westbound, take exit 45 for Log Lake Rd. and go north to US 90. Turn left (west) and go 8.7 mi. to Deaton Bridge Rd.

Open year round, 8 AM to sundown. (850) 983-5363
www.foridastateparks.org/blackwaterriver

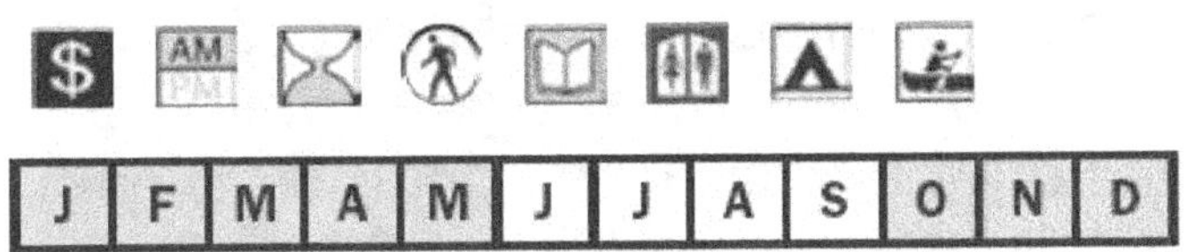

16 Blackwater Fisheries Center

County: Santa Rosa

Nearest city: Holt

Physical address: 8384 Fish Hatchery Rd., Holt, 32564

Coordinates: 30.729556° N, -86.802542° W
Gazetteer page: 27
Size: 590 acres

Nestled in the Blackwater River State Forest's uplands, this ish hatchery is an oasis of wading birds and shorebirds. Stop at the entrance kiosk to check the sightings log and to pick up a checklist. Walk the dikes between the aquaculture ponds, looking for winter waterfowl such as Ring-necked Ducks, Blue-winged Teal and Wilson's Snipe at the muddy edges. Wintering shorebirds include both yellowlegs, Spotted, Solitary and Pectoral Sandpipers, and Semipalmated Plovers. Forster's Terns, Purple Martins and Northern Rough-winged Swallows skim over the ponds. Northern Bobwhites and Wild Turkeys are common in the adjacent forest and wooded ields. Ask at the ofice if you'd like a facility tour, and also if hunting or prescribed ire would prohibit your birding in the woods of the state forest's Carr Unit to the northeast. Bachman's Sparrows sing here in spring and Henslow's Sparrows occasionally overwinter.

Directions: From I-10 eastbound, take exit 31 for SR 87 and head north to US 90/SR 10. Turn right (east) and drive 13.9 mi. to Cooper Ln. outside of Holt. Turn left (north) and go 0.1 mi. to Johns Rd. Turn left (west) and follow Johns Rd./Bryant Bridge Rd. (name change) for 3 mi. The entrance is on the right (northeast) side of the road. From I-10 westbound, take exit 45 for Log Lake Rd. and go north to US 90/SR 10. Turn left (west) and drive 0.5 mi. Turn right (north) on Cooper Ln. After 0.1 mi., turn left on Johns Rd./Bryant Bridge Rd. The entrance is 3 mi. ahead on the right.

Open 7:30 AM to 4 PM, Mon.–Fri.; weekends by appointment only (requires at least 2 weeks advance notice). (850) 957-6177
MyFWC.com/viewing/recreation/wmas/cooperative/blackwater

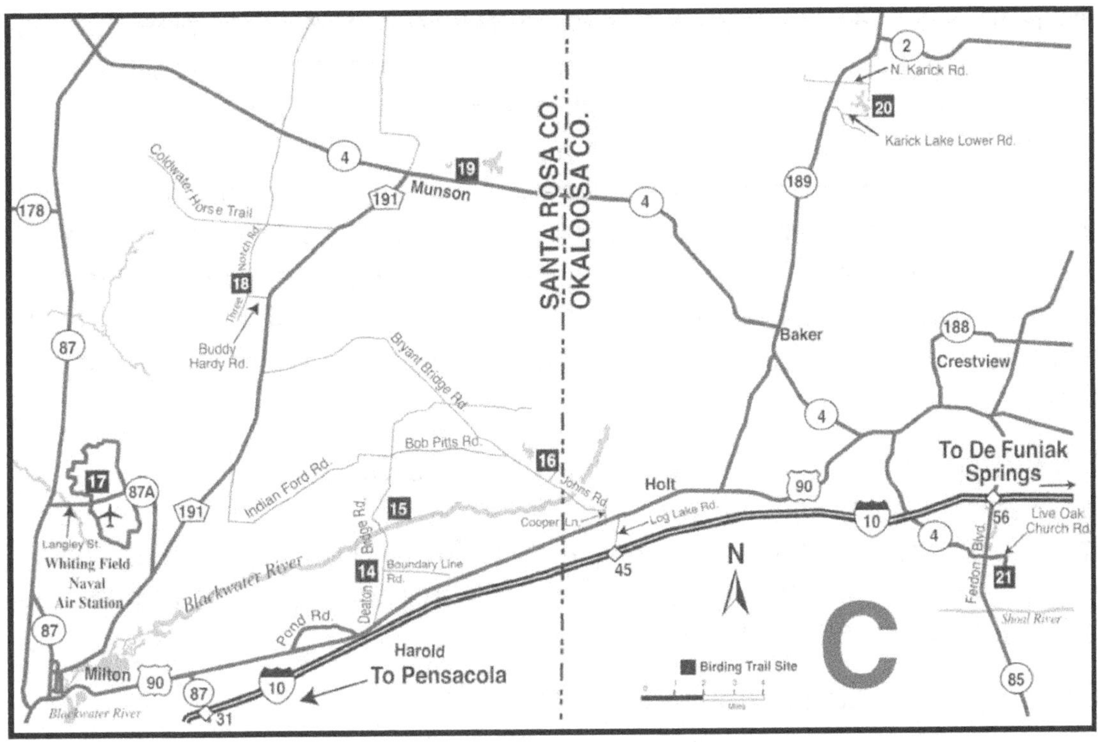

17	## Naval Air Station Whiting Field: Clear Creek Nature Trail

County: Santa Rosa

Nearest city: Milton

Physical address: Langley St., Milton, 32570

Coordinates: 30.707410° N, -87.032045° W

Gazetteer page: 27

Size: 80+ acres

As it descends through mixed pine-oak uplands, this interesting 1.5-mile trail (round trip) leads to a creek, beaver pond and associated wetlands (look carefully for the Atlantic white cedars). Listen for Red-breasted Nuthatches in fall in the uplands and Hermit Thrushes overwintering. At the water, Common Yellowthroats scold from brushy tangles and wading birds like Little Blue Herons and Least Bitterns are possible among the pitcher plants visible from the boardwalk. Listen for Barred Owl, and Prothonotary and Hooded Warblers, all of which breed here. Be alert for Common Nighthawk, Brown Thrasher, White-throated Sparrow and other wildlife species like Southeastern Slimy Salamander, Gopher Tortoise and American Beaver. This is part of a functioning military Naval Air Station and occasional noise from aircraft may occur, but don't let that discourage you from exploring this remarkable gem.

Directions: From the intersection of US 90/SR 10 and SR 87/Stewart St. in Milton, head north on SR 87/Stewart St. for 6.0 mi. Turn right (east) on CR 87A/Langley St. and go 1.0 mi. Turn left (north) at Magda Village, just before the entrance gate and proceed 0.2 mi. to the trailhead parking area.

Open dawn to dusk. (850) 623-7602
www.dodpif.org/checklists/naswf.htm

18 Blackwater River State Forest: Three Notch Rd.

(Hardy Rd. to Coldwater Horse Trail)
County: Santa Rosa

Nearest city: Milton

Physical address: Three Notch Rd., Milton, 32570

Coordinates: 30.800828° N, -86.950923° W (south end)
30.832354° N, -86.942892° W (north end)

Gazetteer page: 27

Size: 5 miles

This 5-mile stretch of Three Notch Rd. offers easy, safe roadside pulloffs with Red-cockaded Woodpecker (RCW) cavity trees ringed with white paint, visible from the road. RCWs are most easily seen in breeding season in the mornings, when they emerge from their nest cavities to ferry food back to their waiting young. Frequent prescribed ire keeps this habitat healthy, so obey signs closing the area for this necessary management event. Use caution on area clay roads, which can be slippery when wet. Also check trails north of Coldwater Horse Trail for RCWs, if desired, along the east and west sides of Three Notch Rd. Seasonal hunting takes place at this GFBWT site; please see Sharing Florida's public lands during hunting season for information on dates, regulations and more.

Directions: From Milton, take CR 191/Munson Hwy. north approx. 14 mi. to Buddy Hardy Rd. Turn left (west) on Buddy Hardy Rd., drive 0.7 mi. and turn right (north) onto Three Notch Rd. Drive towards the intersection with Coldwater Horse Trail; pull off on shoulder as desired. Trails criss-cross the area along Three Notch Rd. and Coldwater Horse Trail, from Coldwater Creek to Juniper Creek (south of SR 4 and west of CR 191). Coldwater Horse Trail leads eastward back to CR 191.

Open dawn to dusk. (850) 957-6140
www.freshfromforida.com/Divisions-Ofices/Florida-Forest-Service

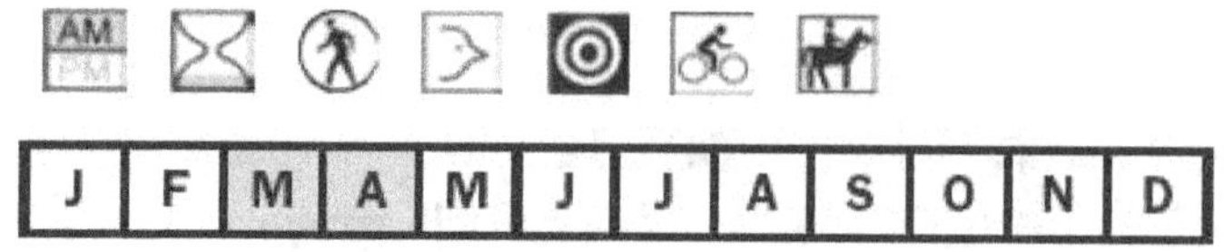

19 Blackwater River State Forest: Bear Lake Loop Trail

County: Santa Rosa

Nearest city: Munson

Physical address: Bear Lake Rd., Milton, 32570

Coordinates: 30.855008° N, -86.838233° W

Gazetteer page: 27

Size: 200 acres

From the camping area, hike the 4-mile trail that rings the lake, watching for migrants like Ovenbirds and Swallow-tailed Kites in springtime. Red-shouldered Hawks echo across the lake and Pied-billed Grebes dive, hunting for ish. Nearby uplands can be good for Chuck-will's-widows and Wild Turkeys. Take water and expect biting insects in warm weather. The lake is popular with anglers in spring and fall. There is no hunting on the trail or in the vicinity of the lake.

Directions: From Milton, take CR 191/Munson Hwy. north to SR 4 in Munson. Turn right (east) on SR 4 and proceed 2.0 mi. to the entrance at Bear Lake Rd. Turn left (north); the parking area is 0.6 mi. ahead.

Open dawn to dusk. (850) 957-6140
www.freshfromforida.com/Divisions-Ofices/Florida-Forest-Service

20

Blackwater River State Forest: Karick Lake

County: Okaloosa

Nearest city: Baker

Physical address: N. Karick Rd. and Karick Lake Lower Rd., Crestview, 32531

Coordinates: 30.905009° N, -86.656031° W (upper entrance)
30.894318° N, -86.660483° W (lower entrance)

Gazetteer page: 28

Size: 3.8 miles

Check these recreation areas for Bachman's Sparrows calling in the sandhills, ducks and wading birds like Green Herons visible from the north access pier, and songbirds like Yellow-throated Warblers and Red-eyed Vireos in the hardwoods around the lake. A 3.8-mile loop trail circles around the lake, traveling along sandhills, gallberry midslopes and hardwood bottoms. Pay attention to ecotones, particularly those edges with hardwoods. These can be good for migrants that prefer this habitat over drier sandhills.

Directions: From Milton, take CR 191/Munson Hwy. north to SR 4 in Munson and turn right (east). Follow SR 4 to its intersection with SR 189 in Baker and turn left (north). The south access (Karick Lake Lower Rd.) is 8 mi. ahead on the right. The north access (N. Karick Rd.) is 0.8 mi. farther north. Hikers must park in designated areas only.

Open dawn to dusk. (850) 957-6140
www.freshfromforida.com/Divisions-Ofices/Florida-Forest-Service

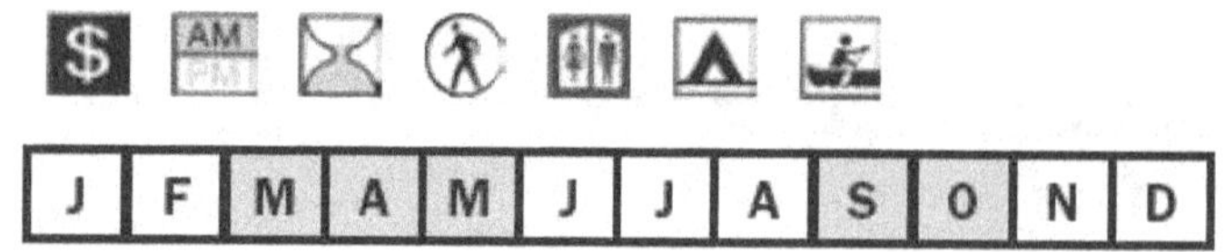

21   Shoal River Wayside Park (Bill Duggan Jr. Park)

County: Okaloosa
Nearest city: Crestview
Physical address: 4502 Live Oak Church Rd., Crestview, 32539
Coordinates: 30.698772° N, -86.570501° W
Gazetteer page: 28
Size: 5.5 acres

Shoal River Wayside Park is worth a quick check for wading birds at the river and songbirds in the adjacent foodplain forest. In this part of the Panhandle, foodplain corridors along rivers like this create migrant highways through arid turkey oak and sand pine uplands. Check the tree line and understory especially in spring migration for songbirds like Prairie Warblers and well camoufaged Veeries.

Directions: From I-10 south of Crestview, take exit 56 for SR 85/Ferdon Blvd. Go south for 1.8 mi. Turn left (east) at Live Oak Church Rd. and go 0.1 mi. Turn right (southwest) and continue on Live Oak Church Rd. for 0.1 mi. Turn left (south) into the park.

Open dawn to dusk. (850) 689-5084, (850) 689-5772
www.co.okaloosa.f.us

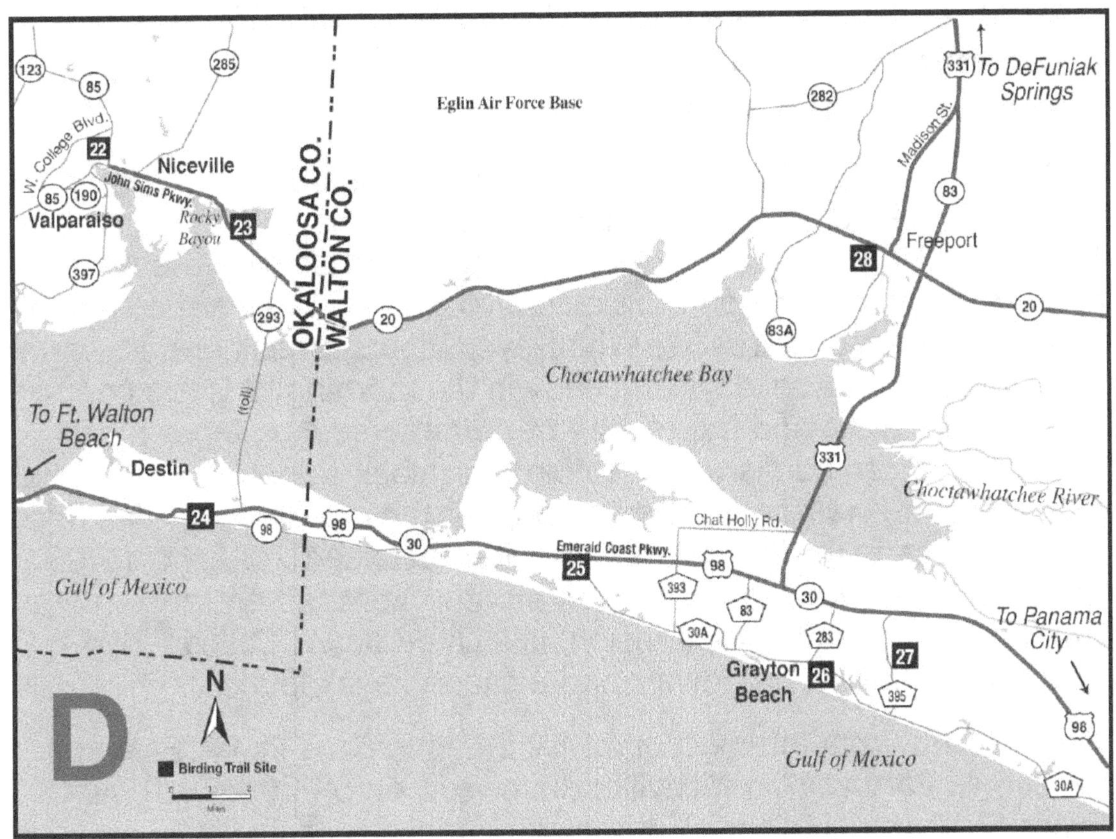

Map D

Choctawhatchee Cluster

22 **Turkey Creek Park**

County: Okaloosa

Nearest city: Niceville

Physical address: 340 John Sims Pkwy. West, Niceville, 32578

Coordinates: 30.523676° N, -86.497348° W (main entrance)
30.532572° N, -86.502322° W (Turkey Creek extension)

Gazetteer page: 28

Size: 0.75-mile boardwalk

Walk the scenic 0.75-mile boardwalk along tannic Turkey Creek through a river forest of titi, maple, cypress and bay. Watch for Green Herons stalking minnows on low hanging branches over the water and Anhingas swimming in the creek. Mississippi Kites are common in summer and songbirds like White-eyed Vireos breed here. In warm weather, visit on weekdays and early in the morning: this is a popular swimming access, and the revelry of swimmers riding inner tubes downstream can be disruptive to birding (albeit tempting to partake in!). The boardwalk is ADA accessible, but the city also provides rides on electric carts for the mobility impaired between 7:30 and 11:00 AM on the frst Wednesday of each month. A second entrance, for the North Turkey Creek Extension, is located on W. College Blvd., which has a 900-ft. boardwalk and a canoe/kayak launch.

Directions: From intersection of SR 20/John Sims Pkwy. East and SR 285/N. Partin Dr. in Niceville, drive west on SR 20 for 1.0 mi. to Evans St. Turn right (north); the park entrance is immediately on your left. From the intersection of SR 190/Valparaiso Pkwy. and SR 397/John Sims Pkwy. in Valparaiso, go north on John Sims Pkwy. for 1.3 mi. across the bridge to Evans St. Turn left (north) and immediately left again into the parking lot. To access the new extension, head east from the park on SR 20 to SR 85. Turn left (north) and go 0.9 mi. to W. College Blvd. Turn left (west) and drive 0.6 mi. past the hospital to the entrance on the left (south) side of the road.

Open 6:30 AM to dark, Tues. - Sun.

North Turkey Creek Extension opens at 8 AM.
(850) 642-0072
cityofniceville.org/turkey.php

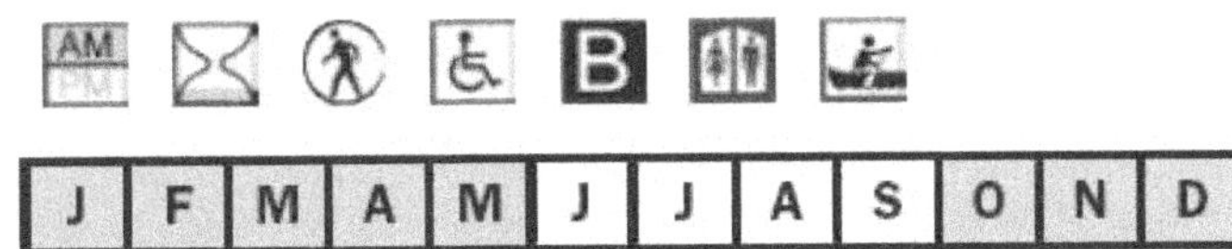

23 Fred Gannon Rocky Bayou State Park

County: Okaloosa

Nearest city: Niceville

Physical address: 4281 SR 20, Niceville, 32578

Coordinates: 30.495944° N, -86.432791° W

Gazetteer page: 28 and 44

Size: 346 acres

This waterfront park is located on Rocky Bayou in Choctawhatchee Bay. Of its three trails, Red Cedar and Rocky Bayou are more interesting for birds than Sand Pine Trail. Walk the trails for migrants like Cedar Waxwings and Indigo Buntings; check the trees in the campground area, too. The waterfront can offer vantages of diving ducks in winter, Ospreys overhead and Spotted Sandpipers on rocky edges in winter. The local Audubon chapter offers bird walks early on Friday mornings – call in advance for details. Loaner optics and feld guides are available.

Directions: From the intersection of SR 285 and SR 20 in Niceville, drive approx. 4.0 mi. east on SR 20/John Sims Pkwy. The entrance to the park is on the left (north) side after crossing Rocky Bayou Bridge.

Open year round, 8 AM to sundown. (850) 833-9144

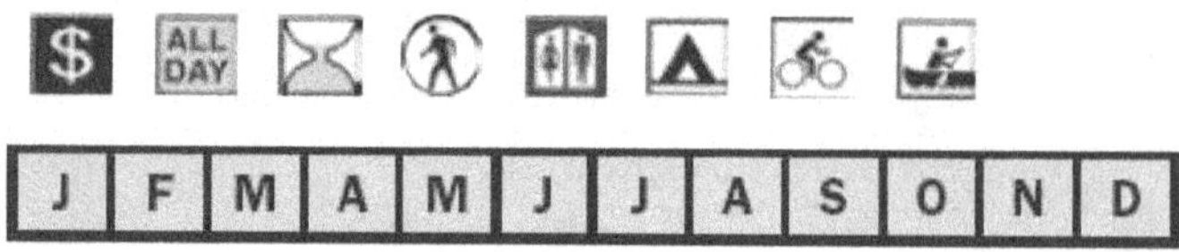

Henderson Beach State Park

24

County: Okaloosa

Nearest city: Destin

Physical address: 17000 Emerald Coast Pkwy., Destin, 32541

Coordinates: 30.386928° N, -86.447520° W

Gazetteer page: 44

Size: 221 acres

Henderson Beach State Park offers nice beachfront for specialties like Snowy Plovers, Least Terns, American Oystercatchers and more. Take care not to disturb beach-nesting birds, which are often cryptic and blend easily with the sand they nest upon. A nature trail by the beach access points winds through a small coastal hammock in a stretch of coastline where little of this important habitat remains. Watch for migrant songbirds here in spring and raptors making landfall or following the duneline in April and October. The campground has some nice trees worth checking as access allows; ask for permission at the entrance gate and be considerate of campers. This site gets busy in warm weather. Loaner optics and feld guides are available.

Directions: From the intersection of SR 293/Danny Wuerffel Way (toll bridge) and US 98/SR 30/Emerald Coast Pkwy. east of Destin, drive 1.5 mi. west on US 98 to the park entrance on the left (south) side of the highway.

Open year round, 8 AM to sundown. (850) 837-7550
www.foridastateparks.org/hendersonbeach

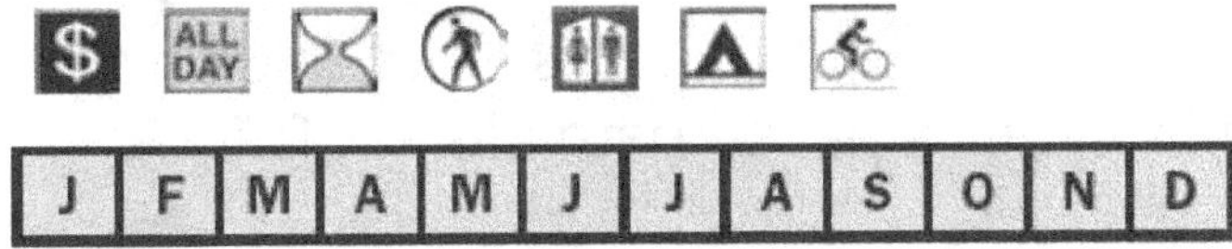

|||||||||||||
| J | F | M | A | M | J | J | A | S | O | N | D |

25 Topsail Hill Preserve State Park

County: Walton

Nearest city: Sandestin

Physical address: 7525 W. CR 30A, Santa Rosa Beach, 32459

Coordinates: 30.371282° N, -86.272744° W

Gazetteer page: 45

Size: 1,643 acres

Topsail Hill Preserve State Park offers 13 miles of inland trails through coastal scrub and past rare, coastal dune (freshwater) lakes. The 2.5-mile Morris Lake Trail is slightly more productive than the Campbell Lake Trail, although either will yield Eastern Bluebirds, Eastern Kingbirds, Red-headed Woodpeckers and Brown-headed Nuthatches, to name a few. Check the beachfront for gulls and Sandwich, Least and Royal Terns. Snowy Plovers nest here, and shorebirds ply the shoals near the outfall for Morris Lake at the Gulf. Scope the surf for Common Loons, Horned Grebes and Northern Gannets winter through spring. The beach is heavily visited in warm weather, so plan accordingly. Educational programs are offered, call for details. Canoes can be rented at the campground store to paddle to Lake Campbell. No outside boats are allowed. Loaner optics are available.

Directions: From the intersection of SR 293/Danny Wuerffel Way (toll bridge) and US 98/SR 30/Emerald Coast Pkwy. east of Destin, drive 8.5 mi. east on US 98 and turn right (southeast) on CR 30A; the entrance is approx. 0.2 mi. on the right (west) side of the road. Cyclists may enter the park via a newly paved path along CR 30A.

Open year round, 8 AM to sundown. (850) 267-8330
www.foridastateparks.org/topsailhill

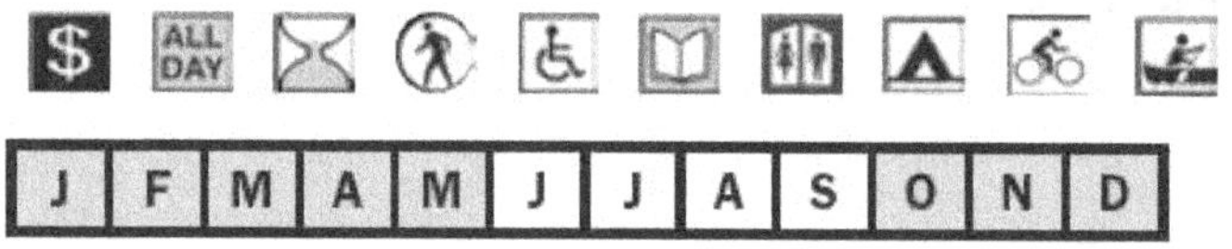

26 Grayton Beach State Park

County: Walton

Nearest city: Point Washington

Physical address: 357 Main Park Rd., Santa Rosa Beach, 32459

Coordinates: 30.334117° N, -86.158050° W

Gazetteer page: 45

Size: 2,227 acres

Grayton Beach State Park is very popular with beachgoers in warm weather, but in cooler months is worth checking. On the north side of CR 30A, the 4.2-mile Grayton Beach Hike and Bike Trail runs through pine fatwoods and along the north end of Western Lake (a brackish, coastal dune lake), which can be good for wading birds, Bald Eagle, Barred Owl, Brown-headed Nuthatch, Pied-billed Grebe and more. For longer hikes, the Lake Loop Trail connects to Point Washington State Forest's (site # 27) extensive trail system. Don't miss the 1-mile, interpretive, Grayton Beach Nature Trail, which begins at the beach parking area. As it winds through sand dunes and under a sand live oak canopy, look for Savannah Sparrow, Eastern Towhee and Orange-crowned Warbler; an additional loop also runs through pine fatwoods (listen for Eastern Bluebird) and along the southern end of Western Lake (check for Common Loon in winter). The beachfront offers plovers, terns and gulls (Bonaparte's in winter) and plunging gannets out to sea October through March. As with all coastal sites, watch for raptors cruising the beachfront and migrants arriving off the Gulf in spring. Loaner optics and feld guides are available.

Directions: From the intersection of US 98 and US 331 east of Destin, drive east approx. 1.5 mi. and then turn right (south) on CR 283. Follow CR 283 for 1.7 mi to CR 30A and turn left (east); the entrance is on the right (south) side after 0.5 mi.

Open year round, 8 AM to sundown. (850) 267-8300
www.foridastateparks.org/graytonbeach

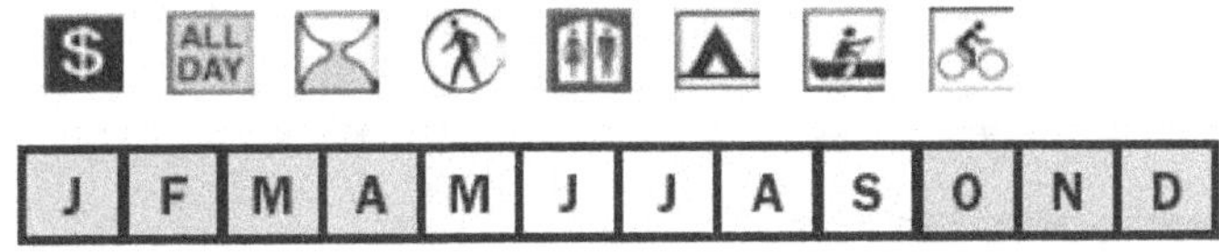

27 Point Washington State Forest

County: Walton

Nearest city: Point Washington

Physical address: S. CR 395, Santa Rosa Beach, 32459

Coordinates: 30.342148° N, -86.131466° W

Gazetteer page: 45

Size: 15,399 acres

Point Washington State Forest offers 3-, 5- and 10-mile hiking loops through longleaf pine fatwoods, coastal scrub and sandhills. Bachman's Sparrows are very likely to be heard singing in spring in areas of wiregrass and palmetto in the southern half of the 3-mile loop. The eastern boundary of this loop crosses the west arm of Peach Creek, where you can listen for songbirds and watch for Red-shouldered Hawks. Cooper's Hawks occasion the fatwoods and Eastern Towhees and Common Yellowthroats are abundant. Trail system connects to Grayton Beach State Park (site # 26) for extended birding adventures. Seasonal hunting takes place at this GFBWT site; please see Sharing Florida's public lands during hunting season for information on dates, regulations and more.

Directions: From the intersection of US 98 and US 331 east of Destin, drive east approx. 3.0 mi. and turn right (south) on CR 395. Trailhead parking is 1.1 mi. on the left (east) side of the road.

Open dawn to dusk. (850) 267-8325
www.freshfromforida.com/Divisions-Offces/Florida-Forest-Service

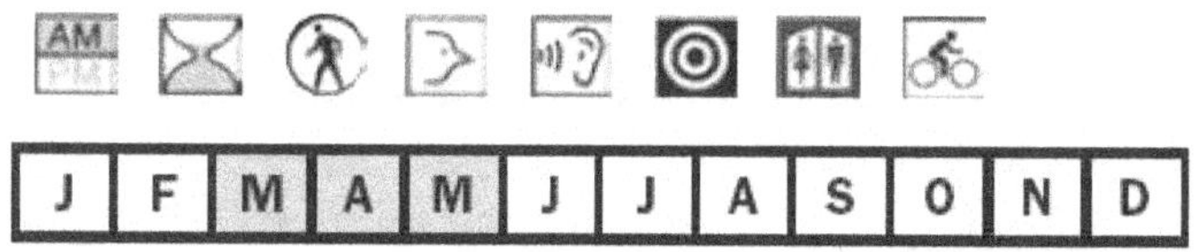

| J | F | M | A | M | J | J | A | S | O | N | D |

---

28 **Harry A. Laird Sr. City Park**

County: Walton

Nearest city: Freeport

Physical address: SR 20 E, Freeport, 32439

Coordinates: 30.501614° N, -86.145701° W

Gazetteer page: 29 and 45

Size: 1.3 acres

This small wayside park has a brief boardwalk along a creek lined with hardwoods. The area is worth checking in migration only, for songbirds like waterthrushes and Worm-eating and Hooded Warblers. Weekend afternoons can be busy with picnickers and playground visitors, but weekdays are left for you and the birds.

Directions: From the intersection of US 331/SR 83 and SR 20 in Freeport, the entrance is 1.6 mi. west on the south side of SR 20 (past Tucker Town Rd.).

Open dawn to dusk. (850) 835-2822
www.freeportforida.gov

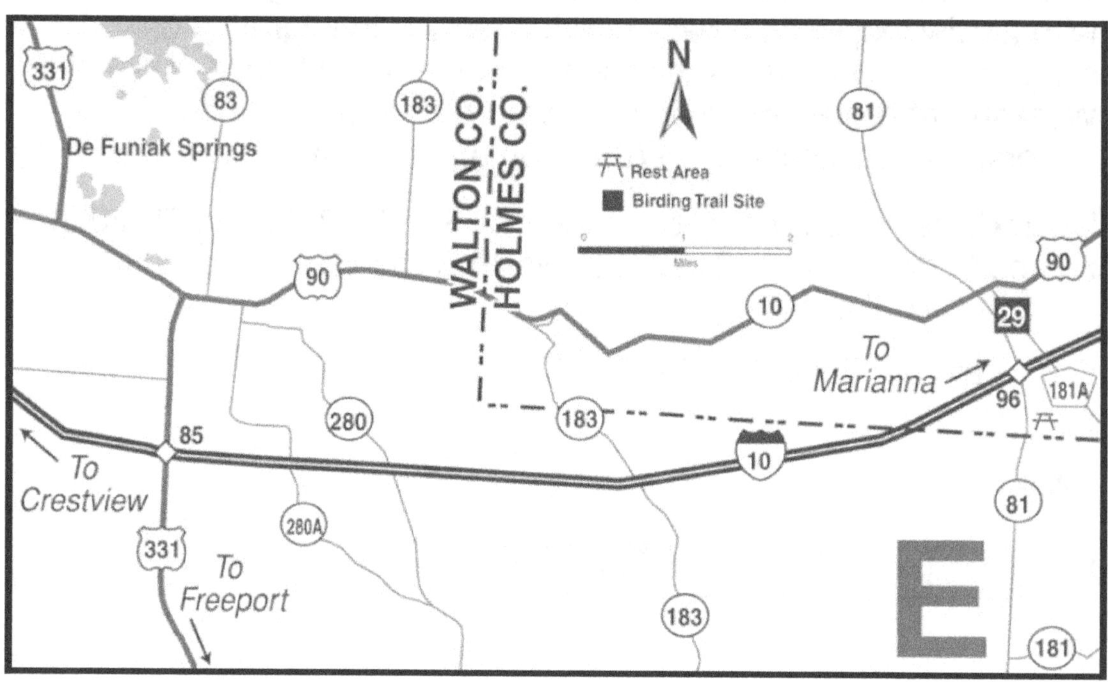

Map E
Dogwood Cluster

29 Ponce de Leon Springs State Park

County: Holmes

Nearest city: Ponce de Leon

Physical address: 2860 Ponce de Leon Springs Rd., Ponce de Leon, 32455

Coordinates: 30.722979° N, -85.930385° W

Gazetteer page: 30

Size: 420 acres

Worth checking in migration, this site's real strength is wintering birds, especially those at the southernmost limit of their range. Birds like Brown Creeper and Golden-crowned Kinglet are possible at this site; your chances improve with your ability to identify birds by sound. Hike both short trails – Spring Run and Sandy Creek – stopping to listen carefully in the shady hardwood forest. This park can be busy with swimmers in warm weather, so weekday and early morning birding may prove the most rewarding.

Directions: From I-10 east of De Funiak Springs, take exit 96 and head north on SR 81 for 1.0 mi. Turn right (east) onto US 90/SR 10; after 0.2 mi. then turn right (south) again onto CR 181A; the entrance is 0.5 mi. on the right (west) side of the road.

Open year round, 8 AM to sundown. (850) 836-4281
www.foridastateparks.org/poncedeleonsprings

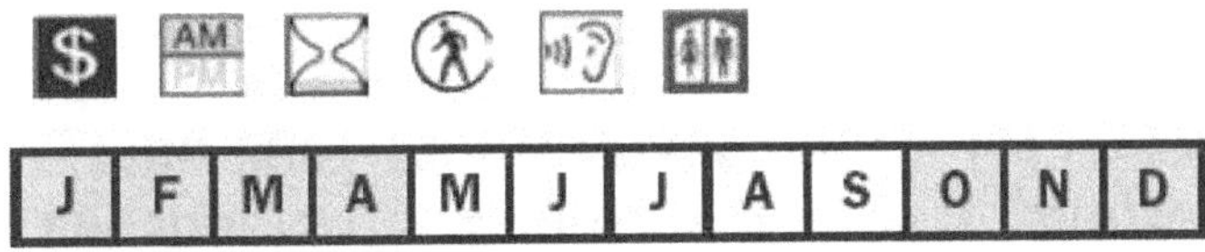

J	F	M	A	M	J	J	A	S	O	N	D

Map F
Kentucky Warbler Cluster

30 Falling Waters State Park

County: Washington
Nearest city: Chipley
Physical address: 1130 State Park Rd., Chipley, 32428
Coordinates: 30.731352° N, -85.529023° W
Gazetteer page: 31
Size: 173 acres

Falling Waters State Park makes for a nice several-hour-long hike, exploring the sinkholes, waterfalls, lake and surrounding uplands via the Wiregrass and Sinkhole trails. Watch for Red-headed Woodpeckers, Bachman's Sparrows, Brown-headed Nuthatches and Summer Tanagers in the uplands and migrant songbirds like Gray-cheeked Thrushes in the leafy understory of dogwood and azalea, beneath the magnolia and white oaks. As always when in this part of northwest Florida, northern species like Dark-eyed Juncos and Pine Siskins are possible in winter. Check for ducks and waders at the lake edge. Scan the butterfy garden for resident and migratory butterfies.

Directions: From I-10 east of De Funiak Springs, take exit 120 and head south on SR 77. After 0.8 mi. turn left (east) onto CR

77A/State Park Rd.; the entrance is 1.7 mi. ahead (road dead ends into park).

Open year round, 8 AM to sundown. (850) 638-6130
www.foridastateparks.org/fallingwaters

31 Florida Caverns State Park

County: Jackson
Nearest city: Marianna
Physical address: 3345 Caverns Rd., Marianna, 32446
Coordinates: 30.808352° N, -85.212422° W
Gazetteer page: 32
Size: 1,279 acres

Florida Caverns State Park has some of the best-preserved uplands in northwest Florida as well as mixed-hardwood swamps lining the drainage basin of the Chipola River. Known for northern species like Red-breasted Nuthatches (in pine forest) and Winter Wrens, this site is ideal for birding with miles of remote trails. Access both the Fish Hatchery Loop Trails and the Pine Island Loop Trails from the Blue Hole Swimming Area. Keep in mind that the Management Trail (part of the Pine Island system) runs north into the Upper Chipola Wildlife

Management Area where hunting seasons will be in effect. Cave tours are available at regular intervals and fill quickly. An onsite canoe concession allows you to access the Upper Chipola River Water Management Area (site # 32). Butterfying is best here in late summer and early fall. Check near the visitor center for the Silvery Checkerspot, which in Florida occurs only in Jackson County. The picnic areas and roadsides have a diversity of swallowtails and sulphurs.

Directions: From US 90/SR 10 in Marianna, head north on SR 166/CR 167/Jefferson St. (becomes Caverns Rd.); the entrance is 2.7 mi. on the left (west) side of the road.

Open year round, 8 AM to sundown. (850) 482-9598
www.foridastateparks.org/foridacaverns

32 Upper Chipola River Water Management Area

County: Jackson
Nearest city: Marianna
Physical address: 3345 Caverns Rd., Marianna, 32446
Bumpnose Rd./Christoff Ferry Lndg., Marianna, 32446
Caverns Rd. at Chipola River bridge, Marianna, 32446
Coordinates: 30.808352° N, -85.212422° W (park entrance)
30.850068° N, -85.259576° W (Christoff Ferry Landing)
30.792445° N, -85.222941° W (bridge)
Gazetteer page: 32
Size: 7,377 acres

For the more intrepid explorer, this rustic river is kept clear enough of obstructions to make a nice day of paddling and birding. Launch from Florida Caverns State Park (site # 31) and paddle upriver toward Christoff Ferry Landing on the Upper Chipola River Water Management Area, where the river forks at the confuence with Waddells Mill Creek. When you're done paddling, foat back watching for brilliant Prothonotary Warblers and Limpkins lurking along the shore. Take water and a map, and allow enough time to return before the park closes at dusk. Christoff Ferry Landing on Bumpnose Rd. is another launch site, but because of its secluded location, the state park is a better choice. You may also launch from the south end of the Chipola River bridge on SR 166/CR 167/Caverns Rd. Seasonal hunting takes place at this GFBWT site; please see Sharing Florida's public lands during hunting season for information on dates, regulations and more.

Directions: The boat launch site is within Florida Caverns State Park: from US 90 in Marianna, head north on SR 166/CR 167/Jefferson St. (becomes Caverns Rd.); the entrance is approx. 2.7 mi. on the left (west) side of the road. Paddle upriver toward Christoff Ferry Landing (B). To reach Christoff Ferry Landing from Marianna, head west on US 90 to Pennsylvania Ave. Turn right (north) and drive 5.2 mi. (name soon changes to Bumpnose Rd.) Turn right (east); the launch site is 0.3 mi. ahead.

Open dawn to dusk. (850) 482-9522, (850) 539-5999
www.nwfwater.com/lands/recreation/area/chipola

Kentucky Warbler

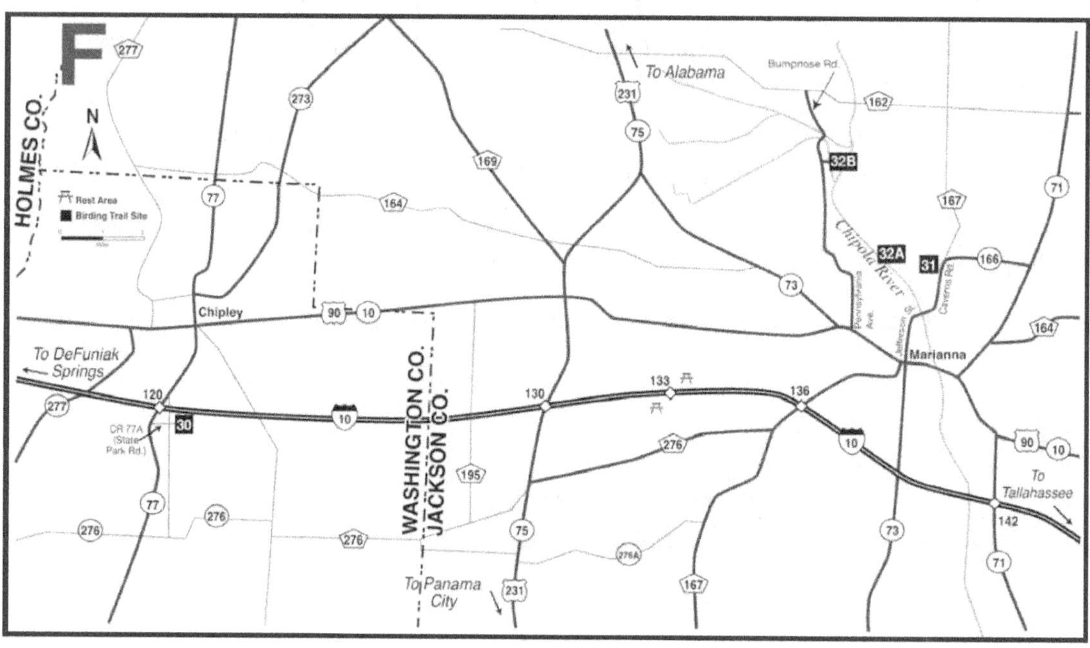

Map G
Indigo Bunting Cluster

33 Pitt Spring Recreation Area

County: Bay
Nearest city: Youngstown
Physical address: Econfina Creek Landing, Youngstown, 32466
Coordinates: 30.431468° N, -85.545768° W
Gazetteer page: 47
Size: 10 acres

This site is part of the 41,000-acre Econfina Creek Water Management Area. As a popular swimming hole, Pitt Spring can be busy on warm afternoons, but in early mornings or on colder days, it offers a nice access to slope/foodplain forest popular with songbirds like Wood Thrushes and Kentucky Warblers. The entrance gate to the small parking area is open daily April through September, and on weekends and holidays October through March. However, interested users are welcome to park outside the gate and enter on foot, to enjoy the trails in the immediate area of the spring. Opposite the spring is a launch point to canoe Econfina Creek. Nearby canoe concessionaires can offer advice on routes and creek conditions; like many Panhandle creeks, the Econfina can be fast fowing and challenging with occasional obstructions that may require portages.

Directions: From US 231 in Fountain (northeast of Panama City), drive 2.0 mi. south and turn right (west) on SR 20; the entrance is approx. 8.2 mi. ahead, on the right (north) side of the highway at Econfina Creek Landing. From Panama City, head northeast on US 231/SR 75 to CR 2301/Blue Springs Rd. Turn left (north) and go 13.0 mi. to SR 20. Turn left (west) and go 0.7 mi. Turn right (north) immediately past the bridge onto Econfina Creek Landing.

Open 9 AM to 7 PM, daily Apr.-Sept.; weekends and holidays only Oct.-Mar. (850) 539-5999, www.nwfwater.com

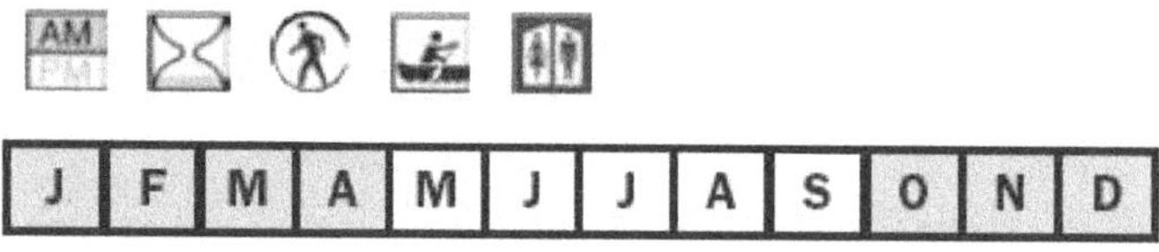

34 Pine Log State Forest

County: Bay/Washington
Nearest city: Ebro
Physical address: 5583 Longleaf Rd., Ebro, 32437
Coordinates: 30.423912° N, -85.881046° W
Gazetteer page: 46
Size: 6,911 acres

Although there are 13 miles of hiking trails at this state forest, the most rewarding birding at this site is via the Campground Loop and Dutch Tiemann Trails accessed from the camping area. The former is marked with red blazes and hugs the cypress margin of a lake for approx. 2 miles. Watch for nesting Pileated Woodpeckers and Prothonotary Warblers, as well as ducks on the lake in winter. The Dutch Tiemann Trail is 6 miles long and stretches south through pinewoods good for Great Crested Flycatchers and Great Horned

Owls, down to Pine Log Creek, and back north to the campground. Take water and sunscreen; bugs may be prohibitive in warm weather. Seasonal hunting takes place at this GFBWT site; please see Sharing Florida's public lands during hunting season for information on dates, regulations and more.

Directions: From the intersection of US 98 and and SR 79 west of Panama City, drive north on SR 79 for 14.1 mi. Turn left (west) on Environmental Rd. approx. 1.0 mi. before Ebro. After 0.3 mi., make the first right (go north) on Long Leaf Rd. and enter the Sand Pine Recreation Area. Park at the campground.

Open dawn to dusk. (850) 535-2888
www.freshfromforida.com/Divisions-Offices/Florida-Forest-Service

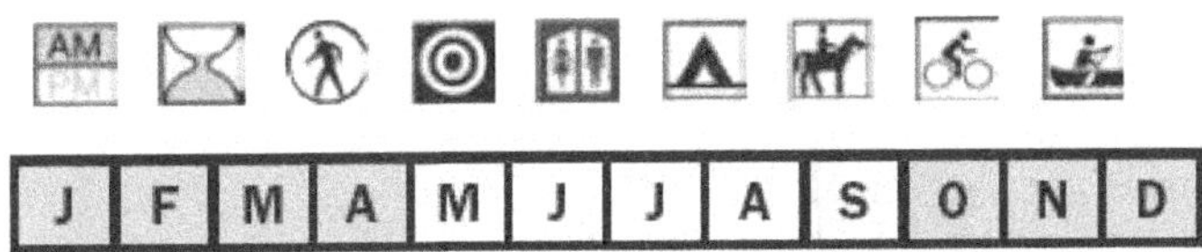

35   Camp Helen State Park

County: Bay

Nearest city: Inlet Beach/Laguna Beach

Physical address: 23937 Panama City Beach Pkwy., Panama City Beach, 32413

Coordinates: 30.275428° N, -85.990431° W

Gazetteer page: 46

Size: 183 acres

Two miles of loop trails are available at this park. The main trail starts at the Rainbow Cottages, runs south across a footbridge, then loops through a coastal live oak hammock and dune system. A path from the loop's south end leads to beachfront where Black Terns are possible in summer, Black-bellied and Piping Plovers in winter. Least Terns and Snowy Plovers have nested in the park. A spur trail runs from the loop's east side to Lake Powell, one of the largest coastal dune lakes in Florida. Coastal dune lakes are rare and in the U.S., occur only on the Gulf Coast. Salt and freshwater mixing at this inlet offers productive feeding for terns year-round, and wintering ducks like Redheads. Loaner optics are available.

Directions: The entrance is on the south side of US 98, 7.0 mi. west of SR 79/N. Arnold Rd., on the west side of the Phillips Inlet bridge.

Open year round, 8 AM to sundown. (850) 233-5059
www.foridastateparks.org/camphelen

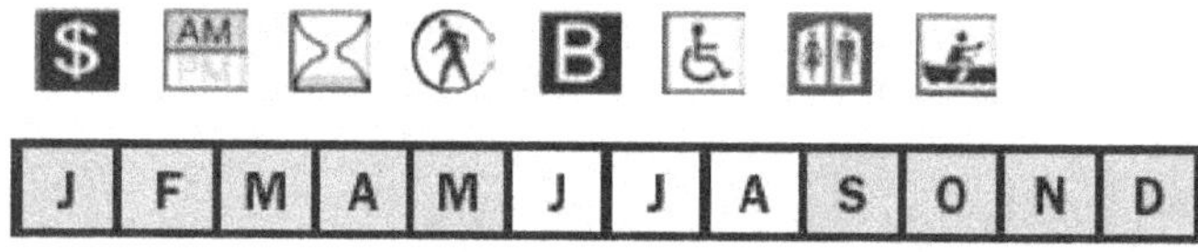

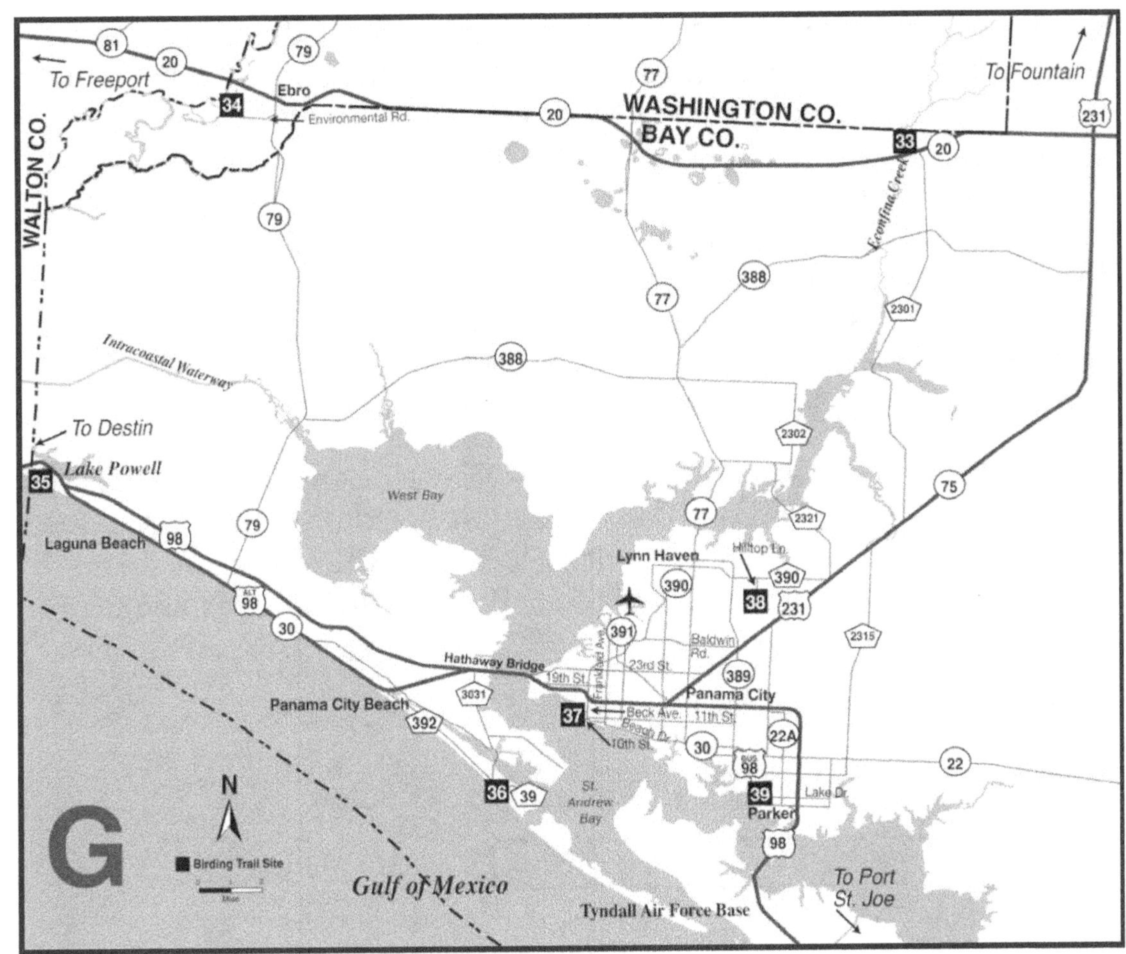

<table>
<tr><td>36</td><td>St. Andrews State Park</td></tr>
</table>

36 — St. Andrews State Park

County: Bay

Nearest city: Panama City Beach

Physical address: 4607 State Park Ln., Panama City, 32408

Coordinates: 30.135113° N, -85.742506° W

Gazetteer page: 46

Size: 1,169 acres

Scan the Gulf from the end of the fishing pier on the peninsula's south (Gulf) side for Brown Pelicans, Least Terns and gulls in warmer months, and gannets plunging near the shore in winter. At the peninsula's east end, beaches north of the jetty fishing area are productive for shorebirds like Snowy Plovers and Willets; Black Skimmers occasionally loaf here. Gator Lake hosts a heron rookery in spring (Great Blue Herons, Great and Snowy Egrets). Check the Buttonbush Marsh Overlook adjacent to the boat parking for Least Bitterns and Wood Ducks. Pine fatwoods throughout are home to Brown Thrashers, Loggerhead Shrikes and Eastern Towhees.

Directions: In Panama City, take US 98 west across the Hathaway Bridge to CR 3031/Thomas Dr. and turn left (south). Follow CR 3031 to its end at the intersection with CR 39 and CR 392. Bear left (straight) onto CR 39/State Park Ln.; the site entrance is ahead.

Open year round, 8 AM to sundown. (850) 233-5140
www.foridastateparks.org/standrews

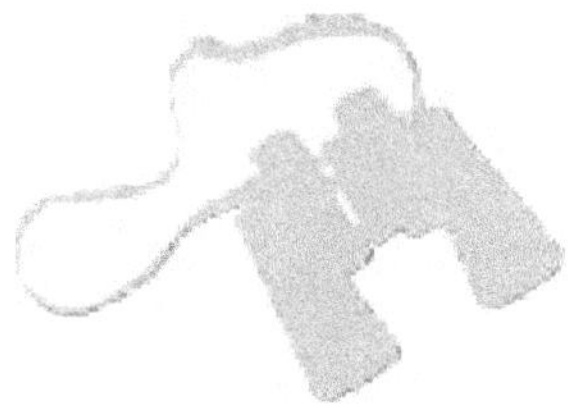

<table>
<tr><td>37</td><td colspan="12">St. Andrews Bird Trail/Oaks By the Bay Park</td></tr>
</table>

County: Bay
Nearest city: Panama City
Physical address: 2701 W 10th St., Panama City, 32401

Coordinates: 30.167245° N, -85.701504° W
Gazetteer page: 46
Size: 5 acres

Particularly rewarding for beginners, this small marina is worth a quick stop if you're in the area. The waterfront boardwalk (west-facing) has a series of educational signs on the area's more common birds like Double-crested Cormorants, Brown Pelicans, herons and egrets. The boardwalk ends at Oaks By the Bay Park to the south, where oaks can be attractive for warblers in April and October. A dune walkover here provides access to the beachfront, for chance encounters with shorebirds like yellowlegs and Dunlin, as well as terns, diving ducks and loons on the bay in winter.

Directions: From US 98 in Panama City, head south on Beck Ave. to its intersection with 10th St. Park your vehicle at Oaks By The Bay Park (directly across 10th St. from this intersection) or turn right (west) on 10th St. and park at St. Andrews Marina.

Open daily, dawn to dusk. (850) 872-3199
www.historicstandrews.com
www.pcgov.org

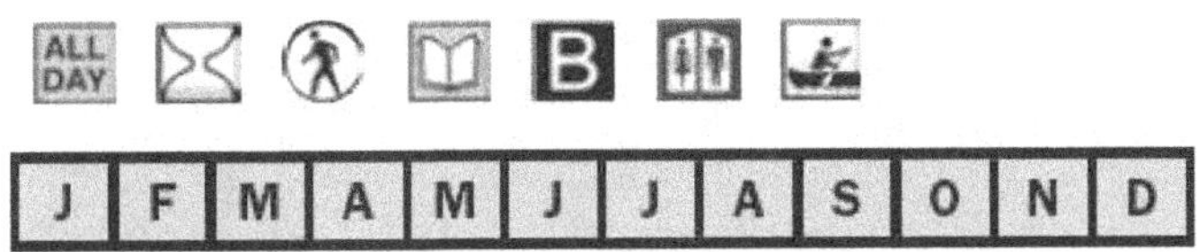

38 Lynn Haven Sports Complex and Nature Trail

County: Bay
Nearest city: Lynn Haven
Physical address: 2201 Recreation Dr., Panama City, 32405
Coordinates: 30.229328° N, -85.615548° W

Gazetteer page: 47

Size: 60 acres

This complex of ball fields yields more birds than you might think, due in large part to the adjacent lake and nature trail. On the lake on the east side of the complex, check for wintering ducks like Ring-necked and Lesser Scaup; a Ross's Goose has wintered here recently. Next, follow the trail east of the lake, along the boardwalk through a small bayhead. Some large trees in this mature wetland hammock make for interesting focks of migrants in October and April. Brushy areas north of the lake, and on the west and south perimeters of the complex may be good for wintering sparrows. Loaner optics and field guides are available.

Directions: From the intersection of CR 390 and US 231/SR 75 in Lynn Haven, drive west on CR 390 for 2.2 mi to Hilltop Ln. Turn left (south); at the end of Hilltop Ln., turn left (east) onto Recreation Dr. Park at the lake on the east side of the complex.

Open 24 hours/day. (850) 271-5547
www.cityofynnhaven.com/leisure/sportscomplex.htm

39 Parker Environmental Exploratorium Park

County: Bay
Nearest city: Panama City
Physical address: 4700 Lake Dr., Panama City, 32404
Coordinates: 30.134811° N, -85.606771° W
Gazetteer page: 47

Size: 5 acres

This delightful little town park offers a waterfront pier with views of Ospreys, Yellow-crowned Night-Herons, Purple Martins and Least Terns, among others. Walk the park's brief trail for more common woodland species such as Carolina Wrens, White-throated Sparrows, Chimney Swifts and Great Crested Flycatchers. A butterfy garden on site is worth checking for occasional Ruby-throated Hummingbirds, as well as butterfies like buckeyes and Gulf Fritillaries.

Directions: From the intersection of US 98 and SR 22 east of Panama City, drive south on US 98 for 1.25 mi. to Lake Dr. and turn right (west). The parking lot at Martin Lake is 0.9 mi. ahead.

Open dawn to dusk. (850) 871-4104
webapps.dep.state.f.us/DslParks/

Wilson's Plover

Baltimore Oriole

Map H
Cape Cluster

| **40** | **St. Joseph Bay State Buffer Preserve: Deal Tract** |

County: Gulf

Nearest city: Port Saint Joe

Physical address: Cape San Blas Rd./CR 30E, Port Saint Joe, 32456

Coordinates: 29.683711° N, -85.367049° W

Gazetteer page: 59

Size: 200 acres

Located on the bay side of St. Joseph Peninsula, this parcel offers a casual hike through sand pine scrub to a fork in the trail. To the right, follow the trail to a large tower and dock overlooking St. Joseph Bay, where you can scope for ducks on the bay, shorebirds along the edges and raptors migrating in October. To the left at the fork, the trail leads to a hardwood hammock with potential for spring songbird migrants like Hooded Warblers. Remember, migrants in this part of the state can make landfall after 11 AM, so don't abandon a site too early! Biting insects can be ferce and the trails offer little shade: bring insect repellent and drinking water.

Directions: From Port St. Joe, take US 98/US 319/SR 30 east (head south) approx. 2 mi. Turn right (south) on SR 30A, drive 6.7 mi. and turn right (west) on SR 30E/Cape San Blas Rd.; the entrance and parking are 4.1 mi. on the right (east) side of the road.

Open dawn to dusk. (850) 229-1787
www.dep.state.f.us/coastal/sites/

41 St. Joseph Peninsula State Park

County: Gulf

Nearest city: Port Saint Joe

Physical address: 8899 Cape San Blas Rd., Port Saint Joe, 32456

Coordinates: 29.744652° N, -85.395420° W

Gazetteer page: 59

Size: 2,716 acres

Because of its peninsular shape and position sheltering a large stretch of coastline from the Gulf, this property is a remarkable migratory hotspot for raptors, songbirds and even butterfies and dragonfies in fall! Hike the spring beaches for Snowy and Piping Plovers (with caution not to disturb them); watch for gannets plunging offshore in fall and winter, and loons, cormorants and ducks wintering in the surf and bay. Check the interior of the peninsula for songbird migrants like Black-throated Blue and Chestnut-sided Warblers making landfall in April. Raptors like Broad-winged Hawks and Swallow-tailed Kites start arriving off the Gulf in late Feb. and March. Canoe concessionaires are available outside the park. Permits are available for after-hours access; camping is allowed by reservation. Loaner optics and feld guides are available.

Directions: From Port St. Joe, take US 98/US 319/SR 30 east (head south) approx. 2 mi. Turn right (south) on SR 30A, drive 6.7 mi. and turn right (west) on SR 30E; the entrance is 8.5 mi. ahead.

Open 8 AM to sundown. (850) 227-1327
www.foridastateparks.org/stjoseph

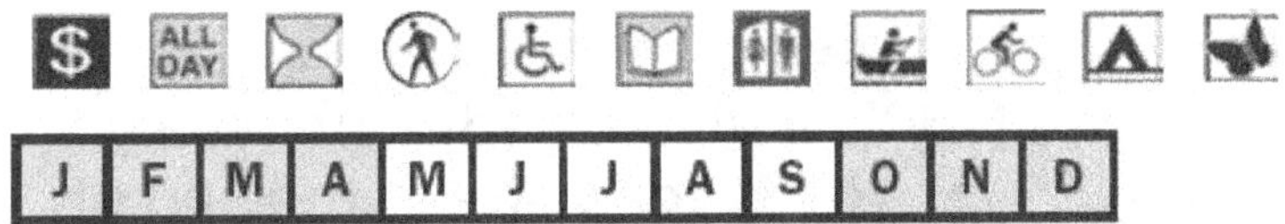

42 St. Vincent National Wildlife Refuge

County: Franklin

Nearest city: Port Saint Joe

Physical address: Indian Pass Rd./CR 30B, Port Saint Joe, 32456

Coordinates: 29.683374° N, -85.222347° W
Gazetteer page: 60
Size: 12,358 acres

This extremely rustic refuge is under-birded in large part because it takes some effort to access it. Cross Indian Pass either by the private ferry or with your own boat. This barrier island is very large: prepare to hike the extensive sand roads or bring a bike. Be sure to pick up a map at the refuge offce in Apalachicola, at the Indian Pass boat ramp, or download one online, and don't forget water and bug spray! Never fear though, your hard work will be repaid: Seaside Sparrows populate the salt marsh on the east side of the island. Interior wetlands host Least Bitterns and ducks, fodder for Peregrine Falcons and other raptors in migration. American Oystercatchers and a variety of plovers nest on the beach (please respect areas closed for their protection) and the island's hammocks are a haven for returning songbird migrants in March and April. Three- to four-day hunts in fall and winter close the island to other uses; please see Sharing Florida's public lands during hunting season for information on dates, regulations and more. Loaner optics are available.

Directions: From Airport Rd. in Apalachicola, take US 98/US 319/SR 30 west for 5.3 mi. and turn left on CR 30 at the fork. Drive 9.8 mi. and turn left (south) on CR 30B/Indian Pass Rd. in Indian Pass. Follow the road east for 2.9 mi. to the ferry site at the end of the road.

Open dawn to dusk. (850) 653-8808
www.fws.gov/saintvincent/

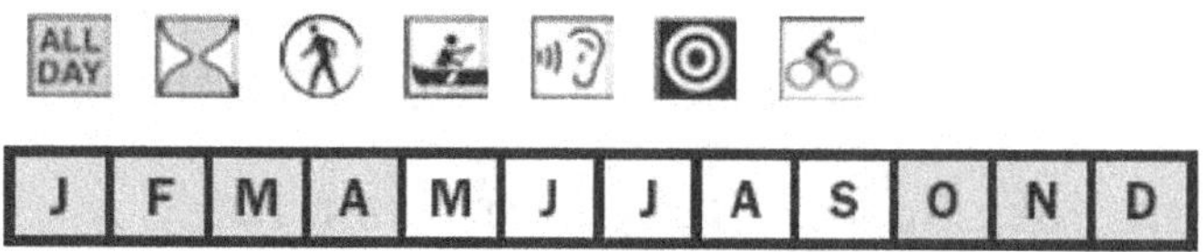

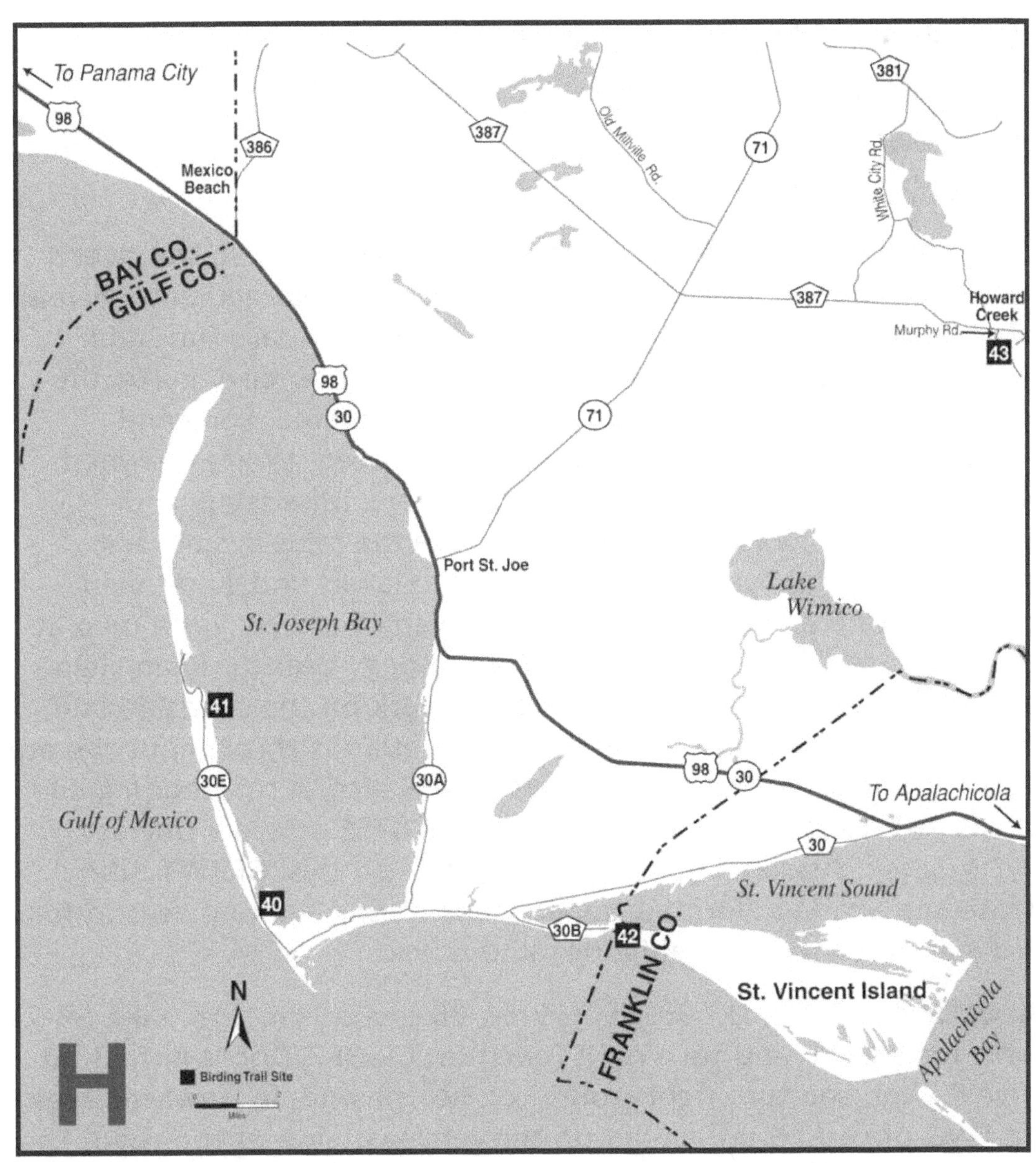

43   Apalachicola River Wildlife and Environmental Area: Old Agricultural Fields

County: Gulf

Nearest city: Wewahitchka/Port Saint Joe

Physical address: S. Murphy Rd., Wewahitchka, 32465
Coordinates: 29.890676° N, -85.069347° W
Gazetteer page: 60
Size: 2,150 acres

This part of the Wildlife and Environmental Area lies on the river's west side, and includes roughly 1,100 acres of old agricultural felds mown and planted for hunting deer, turkey and quail. The same management techniques that beneft these species also make the area prime for sparrows, including the usual Swamp, Song and Savannah, plus the less common White-throated, White-crowned, Field, Vesper and Grasshopper, among others. Mississippi and Swallow-tailed Kites feast on insects above the felds in summer; Southeastern American Kestrels, Cooper's Hawks and Red-tailed Hawks hunt here year round. The best plan of attack: get a map at the offce on the way in and drive Tram, Boggy Branch, Bean Field, Palmetto and Indian Roads. Feel free to park on the roadside and walk the felds for sparrows. Ephemeral wetlands throughout the area are worth checking for wintering waterfowl also. A recreation guide for the ARWEA is available – call (850) 488-8755 or order one at MyFWC.com. Seasonal hunting takes place at this GFBWT site; please see Sharing Florida's public lands during hunting season for information on dates, regulations and more.

Directions: From US 98/US 319/SR 30 in Port St. Joe, take SR 71 north for 9.3 mi. and turn right (east) on CR 387/Doc Whitfeld Rd. Drive 8.2 mi. and turn right (south) on Murphy Rd. in Howard Creek; the FWC offce (0.6 mi. ahead on the left/east side of the road) can provide maps of area roads.

Open dawn to dusk. (850) 827-2934
MyFWC.com/viewing/recreation/wmas/lead/apalachicola-river

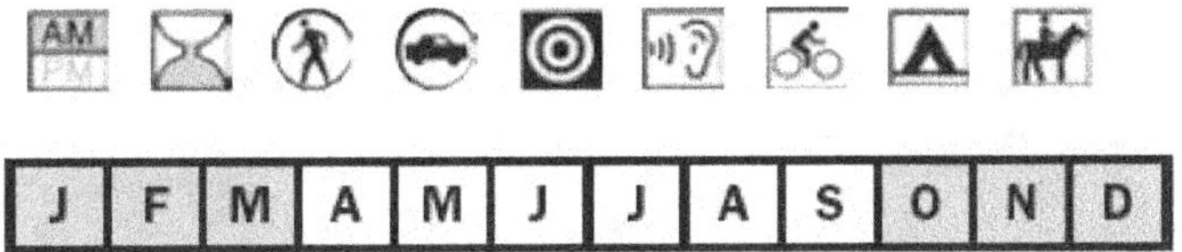

J F M A M J J A S O N D

Map I
Pitcher Plant & Peregrine Cluster

44 St. George Island State Park

County: Franklin

Nearest city: St. George Island

Physical address: 1900 E. Gulf Beach Dr., St. George Island, 32328

Coordinates: 29.684697° N, -84.795493° W

Gazetteer page: 61

Size: 2,023 acres

St. George Island State Park is regularly rated one of Florida's most beautiful beaches, but what all the beachgoers don't realize is that it has spectacular birdwatching too! Bonaparte's Gulls are reliable from winter to spring, Snowy Plovers and American Oystercatchers nest here and Gull-billed Terns cruise the beach in summer. Northern Gannets dive for ish offshore October through April, and spring migrants like Swallow-tailed Kites, Common Nighthawks and Green Herons can be seen arriving off the ocean in March and April. The sandhill trail from the camping area and the oaks surrounding the youth camp are both excellent spots for migrant songbirds like Blue Grosbeaks and Scarlet Tanagers in April. There's something to see year-round, but birding is best and beach visitor numbers are lowest October through April.

Directions: From US 98/US 319/SR 30 in Eastpoint, take SR 300/Island Drive south for 5.6 mi. across the bridge to St. George Island. Turn left (east) on CR 300/Gulf Beach Dr.; the park entrance is 4.3 mi. ahead.

Open year round, 8 AM to sundown. (850) 927-2111
www.foridastateparks.org/stgeorgeisland

45 Apalachicola National Estuarine Research Reserve: Unit 4

County: Franklin
Nearest city: St. George Island
Physical address: E. 6th St., St. George Island, 32328
Coordinates: 29.670753° N, -84.851869° W
Gazetteer page: 60
Size: 75 acres

This small preserve on the sound side of St. George Island is a nice companion to the larger, more well-known migrant fallout site at St. George Island State Park (site # 44). Unmarked trails leading off from the parking area at the end of 6th St. wind through a coastal pine forest and give vantages of the sound and shoreline. Watch for shore- and seabirds like Royal Terns, American Oystercatchers and Laughing Gulls as well as migrants moving through: Common Nighthawks, Scarlet Tanagers, Baltimore Orioles and Swallow-tailed

Kites all pass through coastal areas like these as they arrive off the Gulf each spring. Come prepared with insect repellent and drinking water.

Directions: From US 98/US 319/SR 30 in Eastpoint, take SR 300/Island Drive south for 5.6 mi. across bridge to St. George Island. Turn left (east) on CR 300/Gulf Beach Dr. and go 0.8 mi. to 6th St. Turn left (north) and go 0.2 mi. to the end. Look for a gravel road and small gazebo at the site entrance.

Open dawn to dusk. (850) 670-7700
nerrs.noaa.gov
www.dep.state.f.us/coastal/sites/apalachicola/

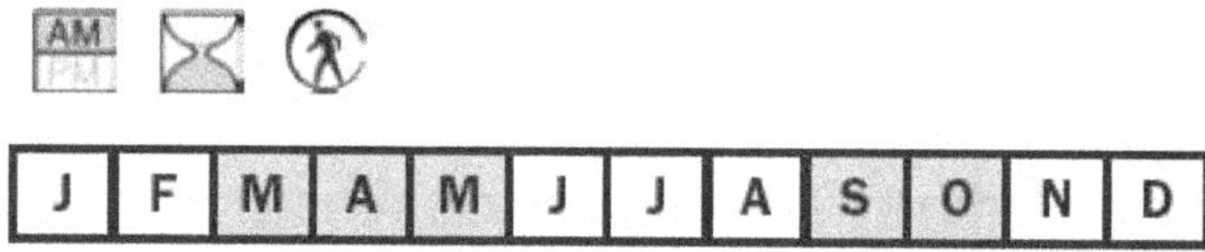

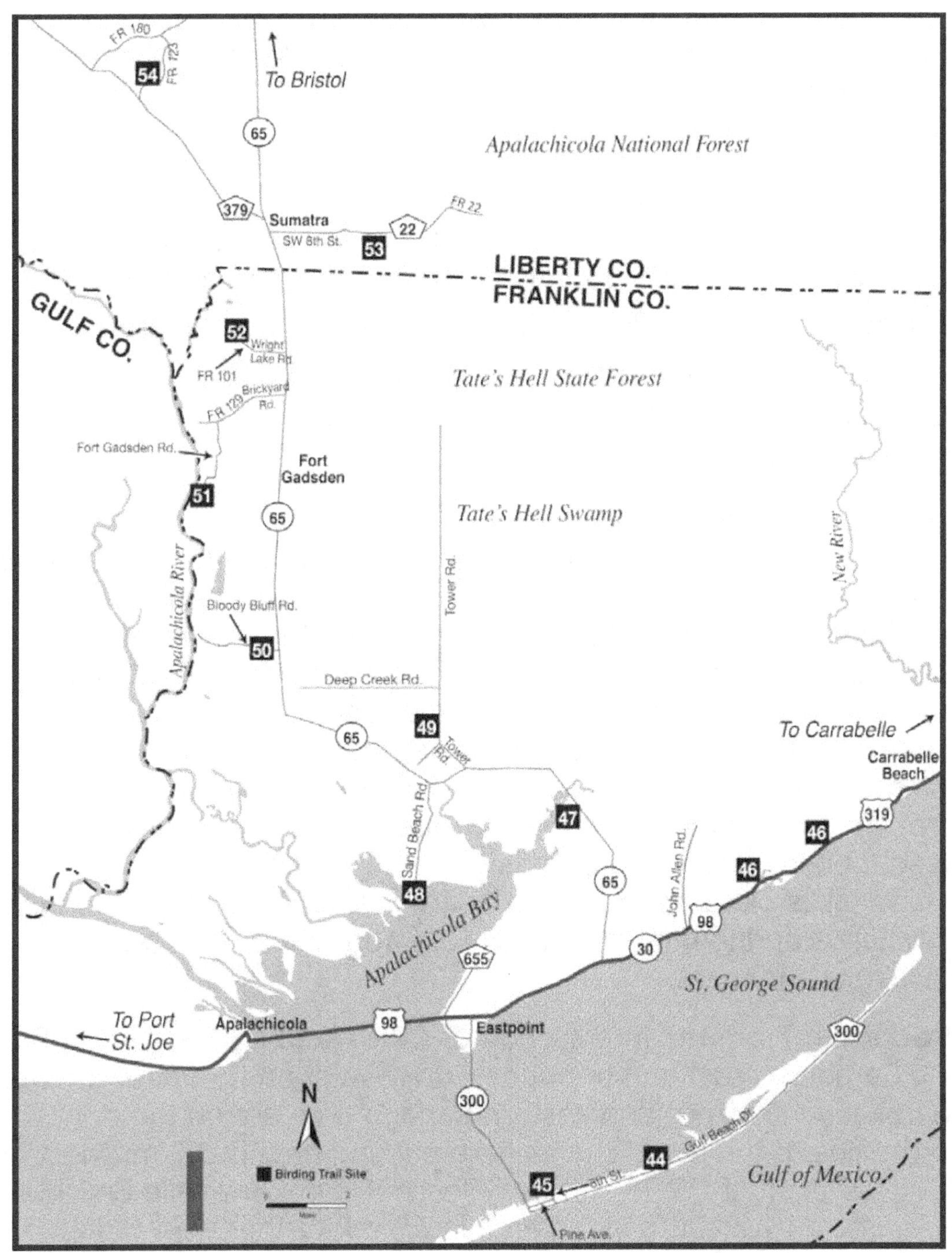

FR 180
FR 123
54
To Bristol
65
Apalachicola National Forest
379
Sumatra
SW 8th St.
22
FR 22
53
LIBERTY CO.
FRANKLIN CO.
GULF CO.
52
Wright Lake Rd.
FR 101
FR 129
Brickyard Rd.
Tate's Hell State Forest
Fort Gadsden Rd.
51
Fort Gadsden
65
Tate's Hell Swamp
Apalachicola River
Bloody Bluff Rd.
50
Tower Rd.
New River
Deep Creek Rd.
65
49
Tower Rd.
To Carrabelle
Carrabelle Beach
47
319
46
Sand Beach Rd.
John Allen Rd.
46
48
65
98
Apalachicola Bay
655
30
St. George Sound
To Port St. Joe
Apalachicola
98
Eastpoint
300
N
300
Birding Trail Site
Miles
Gulf Beach Dr.
44
45
9th St.
Gulf of Mexico
Pine Ave.

46 Tate's Hell State Forest: High Bluff Coastal Hiking Trail 

County: Franklin

Nearest city: Carrabelle/Eastpoint

Physical address: 2381 W. US 98, Carrabelle, 32322 (east entrance) 2985 W. US 98, Eastpoint, 32328 (west entrance)

Coordinates: 29.808446° N, -84.728881° W (east entrance) 29.788651° N, -84.766344° W (west entrance)

Gazetteer page: 61

Size: 4 miles

Catch a glimpse of the vast, 202,437-acre Tate's Hell State Forest on this scenic trail. From either parking area on US 98, a nature trail leads 4 miles through sand pine scrub good for Brown-headed Nuthatches, Red-bellied Woodpeckers and Eastern Towhees year-round. Listen for Yellow-breasted Chats and Orchard Orioles singing in spring/summer. In migration, Summer and Scarlet Tanagers can be found in the pines. Bald Eagles have nested northeast of the eastern parking area, so watch for fyovers! A nice spot for a hike, worth checking in migration. Florida Black Bears live within the forest; look for tracks and other signs along the trail. Seasonal hunting takes place at this GFBWT site; please see Sharing Florida's public lands during hunting season for information on dates, regulations and more.

Directions: From the intersection of CR 67 and US 98/US 319/SR 30 in Carabelle (east end of bridge), drive west on US 98 for 4.7 mi.; the trailhead entrance and eastern parking area are on the right (north) side of the road. The eastern parking area is 3.2 mi. west of the intersection of US 98 and Gulf Beach Rd. in Carrabelle Beach. The western trailhead/parking area is 2.7 mi. further west (south).

From Eastpoint, travel east on US 98; the western entrance is 4.6 mi. east of the intersection with SR 65.

Open dawn to dusk. (850) 697-3734
www.freshfromforida.com/Divisions-Ofices/Florida-Forest-Service

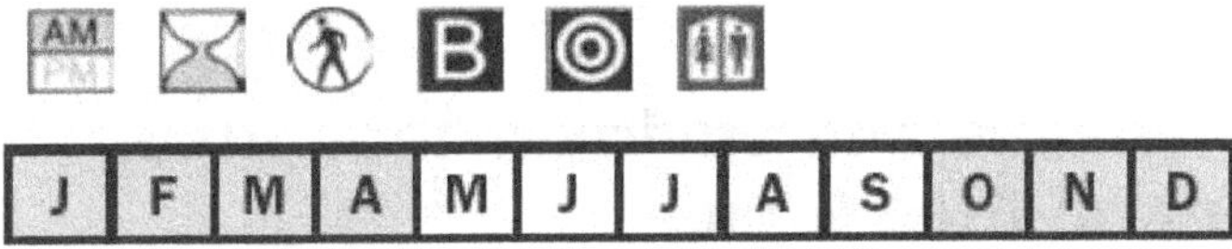

47 Apalachicola River Wildlife and Environmental Area: Cash Bayou

County: Franklin
Nearest city: Eastpoint
Physical address: SR 65, Eastpoint, 32328
Coordinates: 29.819334° N, -84.850006° W
Gazetteer page: 61
Size: 100 acres

If you're traveling between Sumatra and Eastpoint, it's worth taking a moment to pull off at the edge of Cash Bayou to take in the scenery, scan for waterbirds like Bald Eagles and American Bitterns, and check the brief trails for songbirds. Better yet, launch your canoe or kayak from this landing and bird the bayou by boat. A recreation guide for the ARWEA is available – call (850) 488-8755 or order one at MyFWC.com. Seasonal hunting takes place at this GFBWT site; please see Sharing Florida's public lands during hunting season for information on dates, regulations and more.

Directions: From US 98/US 319/SR 30 in Eastpoint, drive east to SR 65. Turn left (north) and go 4.6 mi. Though not well-marked, you may park on the left (southwest) side of SR 65 just before the bridge. Open dawn to dusk. (850) 827-2934

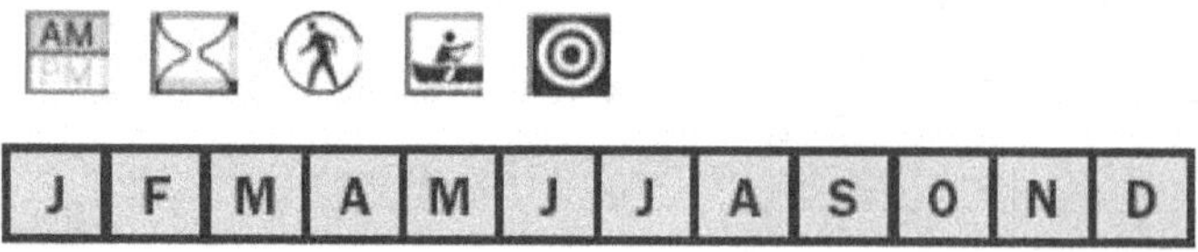

48 Apalachicola River Wildlife and Environmental Area: Sand Beach Tower and Area Roads

County: Franklin

Nearest city: Eastpoint

Physical address: Sand Beach Rd., Eastpoint, 32328

Coordinates: 29.784001° N, -84.910698° W

Gazetteer page: 60

Size: 12,000 acres

Sand Beach Rd. ends at a canoe/kayak launch, pier and viewing tower, in a nice hammock where Yellow-throated Warblers and White-breasted Nuthatches are possible. Scan the reeds for waders like Little Blue Herons and from the tower, scope East Bay for loons, grebes and wintering ducks. Ospreys and Bald Eagles nest in the area, and both Mississippi and Swallow-tailed Kites are likely in summer here in the Apalachicola River basin. The area roads can be interesting birding and butterfying for intrepid explorers, particularly Tank Island Rd. and Butcher Pen Landing. In spring (good) or fall (best), check the fower patches along these roads, particularly at low, wet spots, for marsh skippers such as Broad-winged, Dion, Palatka and Twin-spot. Shallow streams across the road (low water crossings) have irm limestone bottoms, and are not an obstacle to 2WD vehicles, except during very high water. These are a hydrologically sensitive alternative to culverts. Seasonal hunting takes place at this GFBWT site; please see Sharing Florida's public lands during hunting season for information on dates, regulations and more.

Directions: From US 98/US 319/SR 30 east of Eastpoint, drive north on SR 65 for 8.6 mi. Turn left (south) on Sand Beach Rd. to enter the site. An informational kiosk containing maps of area roads is located on the right (west) side of the road. The viewing tower is located 2.8 mi. down Sand Beach Rd.

Open dawn to dusk. (850) 827-2934
MyFWC.com/viewing/recreation/wmas/lead/apalachicola-river

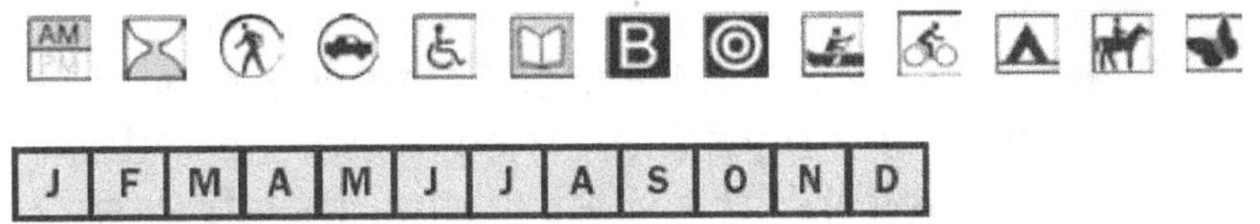

J	F	M	A	M	J	J	A	S	O	N	D

49 Tate's Hell State Forest: Deep Creek Tract

County: Franklin

Nearest city: Eastpoint

Physical address: Tower Rd. and Deep Creek Rd., Eastpoint, 32328

Coordinates: 29.840886° N, -84.903438° W

Gazetteer page: 60

Size: 2 miles

Two miles of dirt roads along the Deep Creek Tract give you quick, easy access to a wet prairie in the Apalachicola River basin. Insect-eating pitcher plants line the ditches around this prairie, which measures several hundred acres. Watching for other recreational users, bird Tower Rd. by foot or from your car, as well as the irst 0.75 miles of Deep Creek Rd., which divides the prairie in two. Watch for typical overwintering wetland sparrows like skulky Le Conte's, Grasshopper and Henslow's, as well as more common Swamp and Song Sparrows. Swallow-tailed Kites use the cypress domes from March to August; wading birds like Snowy Egrets and Little Blue Herons are most concentrated from March to June. In winter, ducks use the prairie's interior and American Bitterns may be seen along the edge; Bald Eagles, hawks and woodpeckers occur year-round. By summer, the sun is punishing and bugs are ierce, hence the state forest's name! Seasonal hunting takes place at this GFBWT site; please see Sharing Florida's public lands during hunting season for information on dates, regulations and more.

Directions: From US 98/US 319/SR 30 east of Eastpoint, drive north on SR 65 for 7.3 mi. and turn right (north) on Tower Rd. After 1.1 mi., bear right (north) at the fork; the site is along the left (west) side of Tower Rd. and south side of Deep Creek Rd.

Open dawn to dusk. (850) 697-3734
www.freshfromforida.com/Divisions-Ofices/Florida-Forest-Service
MyFWC.com/viewing/recreation/wmas/cooperative/tates-hell/

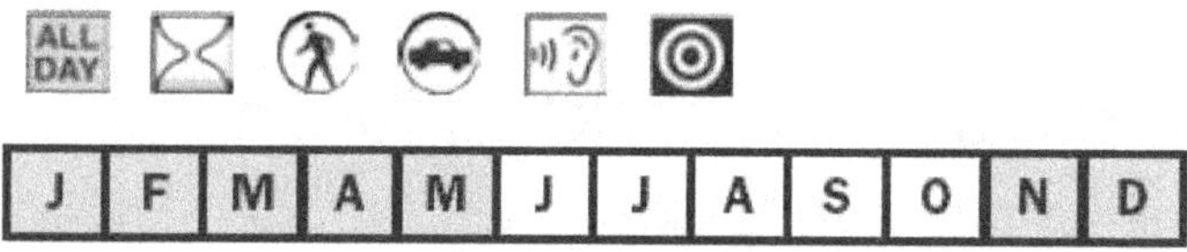

| J | F | M | A | M | J | J | A | S | O | N | D |

| 50 | **Apalachicola River Wildlife and Environmental Area: Bloody Bluff Tract** |

County: Franklin

Nearest city: Sumatra

Physical address: Bloody Bluff Rd., Eastpoint, 32328

Coordinates: 29.869528° N, -84.975057° W

Gazetteer page: 60

Size: 4,800 acres

Along the drive down Bloody Bluff Rd., watch the edges for sparrows including Chipping, Swamp and Song, and listen in spring for Bachman's Sparrows. The river trail near the boat ramp at the end of the road can be good for songbirds like Yellow-throated Warblers and Blue-headed Vireos, and Swallow-tailed and Mississippi Kites frequent the river run. Most roads in this area can be interesting for birding (Creek Rd. and Old County Rd. have been productive for sparrows in the past) and several species of rare plants occur on the area. This site is very rustic and there are some low water crossings on the dirt roads, but these washes are hard bottomed (and accordingly passable in 2WD except in times of very high water). Seasonal hunting takes place at this GFBWT site; please see Sharing Florida's public lands during hunting season for information on dates, regulations and more.

Directions: From US 98/US 319/SR 30 east of Eastpoint, drive north on SR 65 for 14.2 mi. Turn left (west) on Bloody Bluff Rd. to enter the site.

Open dawn to dusk. (850) 827-2934
MyFWC.com/viewing/recreation/wmas/lead/apalachicola-river

51 Apalachicola National Forest: Fort Gadsden Historical Site

County: Franklin

Nearest city: Sumatra

Physical address: Fort Gadsden Rd., Sumatra, 32328

Coordinates: 29.940532° N, -85.007360° W

Gazetteer page: 60

This site of a British fort dating back to the War of 1812 is slowly returning to the nature it was eked out of centuries ago. Fortiications and historical signage are surrounded by the Apalachicola National Forest's fatwoods on one side, good for Common Yellowthroats and the occasional Bachman's Sparrow; on the other side, the shoreline at the broad, brown Apalachicola River is lined with hardwoods and cypress, home to singing Northern Parulas and Prothonotary Warblers. Hike the fatwoods trail from the parking area, and walk the waterfront in migration. Breeding raptors like Red-shouldered Hawks and Mississippi Kites are raucous in spring/summer. Longleaf pines used by Red-cockaded Woodpeckers as cavity trees are ringed with white paint.

Directions: From the intersection of SR 65 and 8th St./CR 22 in Sumatra, travel south on SR 65 for 4 mi. Turn right (west) on FR 129/Brickyard Rd. and follow for 2.1 mi. Turn left (south) on Fort Gadsden Rd. and continue for 0.7 mi. to the site entrance.

Open 8 AM to 8 PM. (850) 643-2282
www.fs.usda.gov/apalachicola

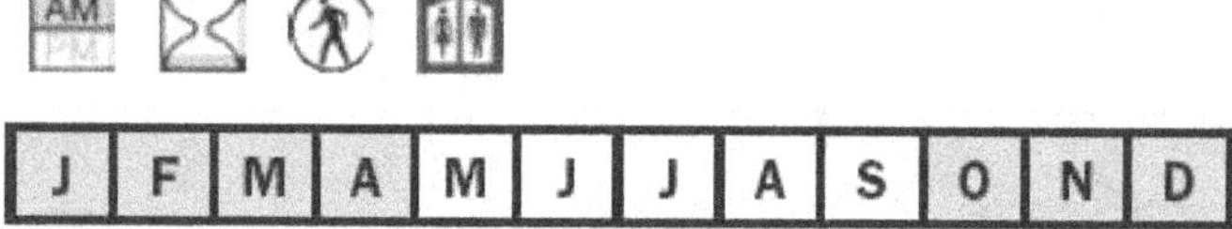

J	F	M	A	M	J	J	A	S	O	N	D

52 Apalachicola National Forest: Wright Lake

County: Franklin

Nearest city: Sumatra

Physical address: NF 101/Wright Lake Rd., Bristol, 32321

Coordinates: 30.000129° N, -85.001991° W

Gazetteer page: 48 and 60

Two trails at this site, a 0.25-mile trail around the lake and a 5-mile one, traverse stretches of basin swamp and longleaf pine-wiregrass community. Plants and animals in the latter community type have come to depend on frequent ire that keeps the understory low and open, stimulating pine seeds to germinate and wiregrass to fower. Since natural ire is feared by people, it's been suppressed in much of Florida, allowing many remaining examples of this community to become overgrown and unsuitable for the animals that are uncompromisingly dependent on it. Here in the national forest, prescribed ire is used to keep pinewoods healthy, making it one of the best places to see Red-cockaded Woodpeckers (RCWs) and Bachman's Sparrows. Spring mornings are best for spotting both, when sparrow males are singing "here, kitty-kitty-kitty-kitty" on their territories, and RCWs are busy coming and going from their nest cavities, carrying food to their young. Seasonal hunting takes place at this GFBWT site along the 5-mile trail; please see Sharing Florida's public lands during hunting season for information on dates, regulations and more.

Directions: From the intersection of SR 65 and 8th St./CR 22 in Sumatra, travel south on SR 65 for 1.9 mi. to FR 101/Wright Lake Rd. Turn right (west) and follow FR 101/Wright Lake Rd. for 1.6 mi. to the site.

Open 24 hours/day. (850) 643-2282
www.fs.usda.gov/apalachicola

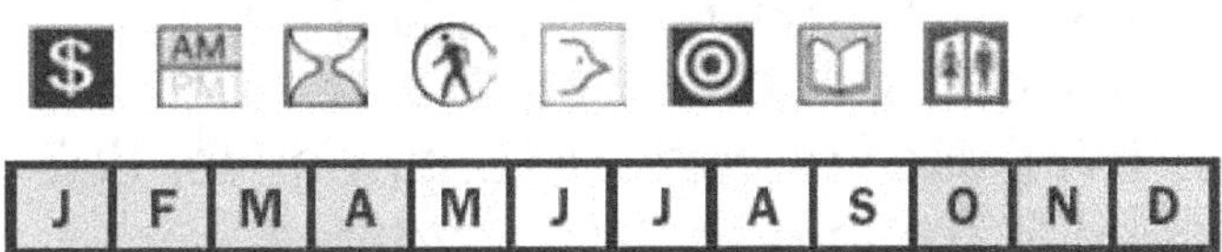

53 **Apalachicola National Forest: County Road 22 Pond**

County: Liberty
Nearest city: Sumatra
Physical address: SW 8th St./CR 22, Bristol, 32321
Coordinates: 30.022150° N, -84.955450° W
Gazetteer page: 48

While there are Red-cockaded Woodpecker (RCW) cavity trees ringed with white paint visible throughout the 571,000-acre national forest, this site offers the opportunity to park and hike to view the birds on foot without danger from passing trafic. From the small parking area, hike south to the small lake where ducks like Lesser Scaup may be found occasionally in winter. The west side of the lake is a good foraging and nesting area for the woodpeckers. Around the cavity entrances, you'll notice sap running from holes drilled by the woodpeckers; this is thought to deter snakes from raiding the nests. Please take care not to approach the cavity trees too closely; these birds are protected by law and harassment is not tolerated. Patient observers will easily see RCWs on spring mornings as they emerge and then begin bringing food to chicks in the cavity; early evenings are good, too. Please stay on the trails to avoid trampling some of the sensitive and rare plants that occur in this area. Seasonal hunting takes place at this GFBWT site; please see Sharing Florida's public lands during hunting season for information on dates, regulations and more.

Directions: From SR 20 just west of Bristol, take SR 12 south for 21.4 mi. to SR 65 in Wilma. Go south on SR 65 for 10.0 mi. to Sumatra and turn left (east) on SW 8th St./CR 22. Go 1.4 mi. down this wide unpaved road (also known as FR 22). A narrow woods road to the site is on the right (south) side. Park on SW 8th St./CR 22/FR 22 and walk the woods road to the pond.

Open dawn to dusk. (850) 643-2282
www.fs.usda.gov/apalachicola

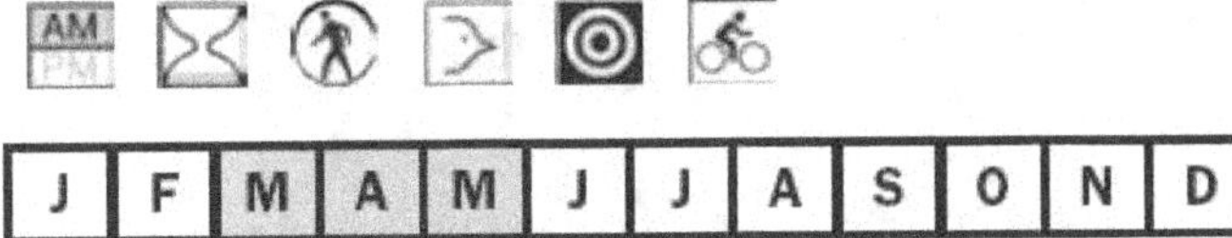

54 Apalachicola National Forest: Post Office Bay, Forest Road 123 Northeast

County: Liberty

Nearest city: Sumatra

Physical address: Forest Roads 123 and 180, Bristol, 32321

Coordinates: 30.089149° N, -85.042806° W

Gazetteer page: 48

Size: 6.6 miles

This 6.6-mile, spectacular scenic drive passes through wet savannas and longleaf pine forest in some of the best condition you'll ind anywhere in the southeast. Watch for carnivorous plants, including four species of pitcher plants, growing in roadside wetlands. Stop at roadside pulloffs to explore, looking for breeding Red-cockaded Woodpeckers, Bachman's Sparrows and Swainson's Warblers. Winter can be good for rarer sparrows like Henslow's and Le Conte's in the soggy fatwoods and savannas. Butterfy viewing is good all year but best in fall. When the blazing stars (*Liatris*) are blooming along CR

379 or the forest roads, visitors may ind impressive numbers and a wide diversity of species. Special butterfies that occur here include Wild Indigo Duskywing, Florida Dusted Skipper and Berry's Skipper. Take care not to trample delicate plant life by walking off trails. Seasonal hunting takes place at this GFBWT site; please see Sharing Florida's public lands during hunting season for information on dates, regulations and more.

Red-banded Hairstreak

Directions: From the intersection of SR 65 and SW 8th St./CR 22 in Sumatra, travel north on SR 65 for 0.6 mi. Turn left (west) onto CR

379. The best access point for FR 123 is 5.9 mi. ahead on the right (east) side of the road. This road can be driven as a loop with stops to view RCW clusters and savannas: drive FR 123 for 3.3 mi. until it ends at FR 180. Turn left (west) and travel FR 180 for another 3.3 mi. FR 180 will return you to CR 379, 1.5 mi. further north of your starting point.

Open dawn to dusk. (850) 643-2282
www.fs.usda.gov/apalachicola

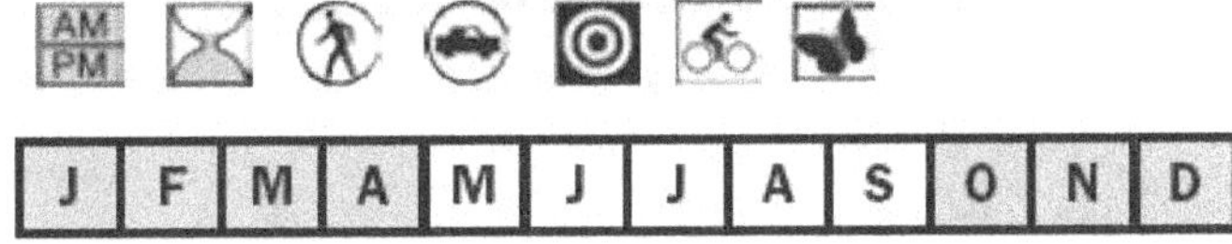

Map J
Bluffs Cluster

55 Apalachicola Bluffs and Ravines Preserve: Garden of Eden Trail

County: Liberty
Nearest city: Bristol
Physical address: Garden of Eden Rd., Bristol, 32321
Coordinates: 30.451730° N, -84.968490° W
Gazetteer page: 48
Size: 6,295 acres

At 135 feet above the Apalachicola River, Alum Bluff is the largest geological exposure in Florida. In fact, the topography of this site feels nothing like what most people expect from Florida. Hike the steep 3.75-mile trail through longleaf pine sandhills, upland mixed hardwoods, along the tops of steephead ravines, down into slope forests, across shallow streams, and out to the bluff. Listen for Wood Thrushes, Hooded Warblers, Barred Owls and Broad-winged Hawks along the way. Butterfy viewing is good in spring and fall. In the dry sandhills, expect Southern Dogface, Cloudless Sulphur and other pierids (whites and yellows), plus various duskywings, including Sleepy and Juvenal's in spring. Also check for Dotted Skipper; in the ravines, search for Spring and Summer Azures and Carolina Satyr. Not for the faint of heart, this hike will make you earn the spectacular views of the Apalachicola River, but they're well worth the effort. Watch your footing and definitely bring water. While there's no hunting on this property, The Nature Conservancy encourages visitors to wear bright colors in season, for safety.

Directions: From SR 20 in Bristol, take SR 12 north for 1.4 mi. Turn left (west) at Garden of Eden Rd. (look for "Apalachicola Bluff-Garden of Eden" sign).

Open dawn to dusk. (850) 643-2756 www.nature.org

56 Torreya State Park

County: Liberty
Nearest city: Bristol
Physical address: 2576 NW Torreya Park Rd., Bristol, 32321
Coordinates: 30.558707° N, -84.949714° W
Gazetteer page: 32
Size: 2,650 acres

This park is named after the Torreya tree, the world's rarest evergreen, which only grows on bluffs on the eastern side of the Apalachicola River. Still in decline, this tree is the subject of much study, and can be seen here, alongside wonderful vantages of the Apalachicola River and interesting birds. The most productive birding spots are the areas of the trail around Stone Bridge, down by the river northwest of the historic home, and on the trails to Rock Bluff Primitive Campground. As in much of extreme north Florida, watch for northern birds like Winter Wren, Louisiana Waterthrush, Golden-crowned Kinglet and Brown Creeper. Brown-headed Nuthatch and Bachman's Sparrow are possible in the sandhills, and the high canopies along the river can be good for Yellow-throated Vireo in spring. Birding by ear skills are very useful here. Spring and fall are ideal times for butterfy enthusiasts to visit. This park is one of the most reliable spots in Florida for Mourning Cloak (early spring). May is good for seeing Banded, King's and Striped Hairstreaks; a fall day can produce more than a dozen skipper species. The park features more than 17 miles of hiking trails and numerous camping options.

Directions: From I-10 west of Quincy, take exit 174 for SR 12 and go toward Greensboro. Stay on SR 12 through Greensboro and continue (approx. 14 mi. total from I-10) until the intersection with CR 1641. Turn right (north) on CR 1641 and continue left (northwest) at the fork with CR 270. Bear right (northwest) at the next fork with CR 270. Bear right at the next fork (CR 1641 becomes Torreya State Park Rd.) and follow the signs to the park entrance. Note: some maps show CR 1641 as CR 271.

Open year round, 8 AM to sundown. (850) 643-2674
www.foridastateparks.org/torreya

J	F	M	A	M	J	J	A	S	O	N	D

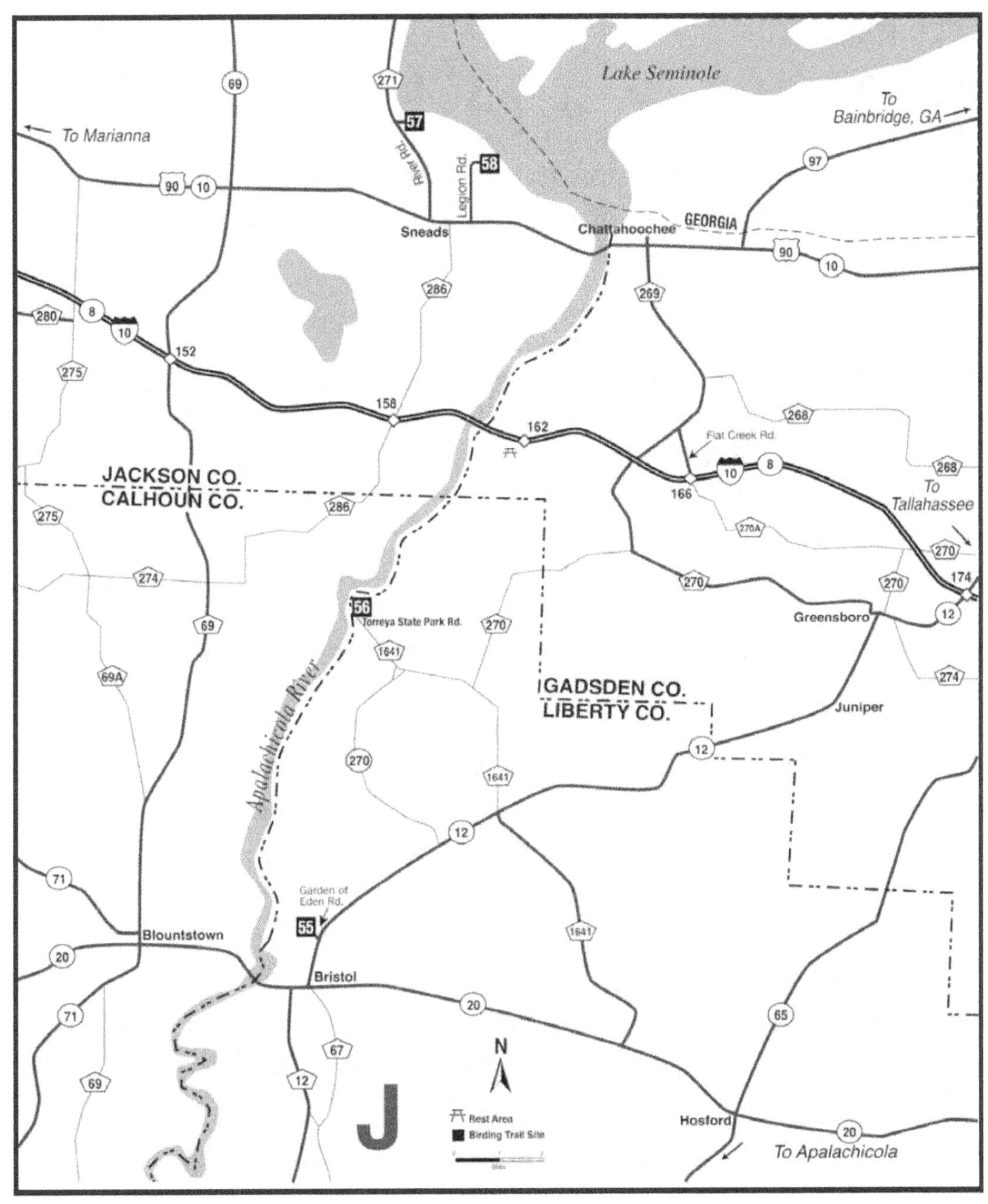

Lake Seminole
69
271
57
To Marianna
58
Legion Rd.
River Rd.
97
To Bainbridge, GA
90
10
Sneads
Chattahoochee
GEORGIA
90
10
286
280
8
269
10
152
275
158
162
268
Flat Creek Rd.
JACKSON CO.
CALHOUN CO.
10
8
166
268
286
270A
To Tallahassee
275
274
270
270
174
56
Torreya State Park Rd.
270
Greensboro
12
69
1641
GADSDEN CO.
LIBERTY CO.
274
69A
Juniper
270
12
1641
71
12
Garden of
Eden Rd.
Blountstown
55
1641
20
Bristol
N
65
71
20
67
12
69
J
Rest Area
Hosford
20
Birding Trail Site
Apalachicola River
To Apalachicola

57   Three Rivers State

Park

County: Jackson
Nearest city: Sneads
Physical address: 7908 Three Rivers Park Rd., Sneads, 32460
Coordinates: 30.739096° N, -84.936161° W
Gazetteer page: 32
Size: 667 acres

Pine and hardwood uplands with big, old trees characterize this park on the south shore of Lake Seminole. This lake is actually a reservoir created at the confuence of the Flint and Chattahoochee Rivers, where they form the Apalachicola—the opposite shoreline lies in Georgia. Bird the Lakeside Trail which begins near the campground, as well as the Half Dry Creek Trail by the picnic area. Habitat and location are good for Kentucky Warbler and Louisiana Waterthrush in spring/summer. Otherwise, wintering birds characteristic of the area, including Red-breasted Nuthatch and Golden-crowned Kinglet are rare but possible in cooler months. In winter, also scope the lake from two birding blinds—you never know what wintering waterfowl you may find! A Yellow-billed Loon wintered on a reservoir south of Atlanta in 2003-04. Who knows what else is out there, simply waiting for birders to find it? Loaner optics and field guides are available at the entrance station.

Directions: From I-10, take exit 158 for CR 286. Head north for 5.2 mi. to US 90/SR 10 in Sneads. Turn left (west) and go 0.4 mi. Turn right (north) on CR 271/River Rd. and drive 2.1 mi. Turn right (east) at Three Rivers Park Rd. The entrance is just ahead.

Open year round, 8 AM to sundown. (850) 482-9006
www.foridastateparks.org/threerivers

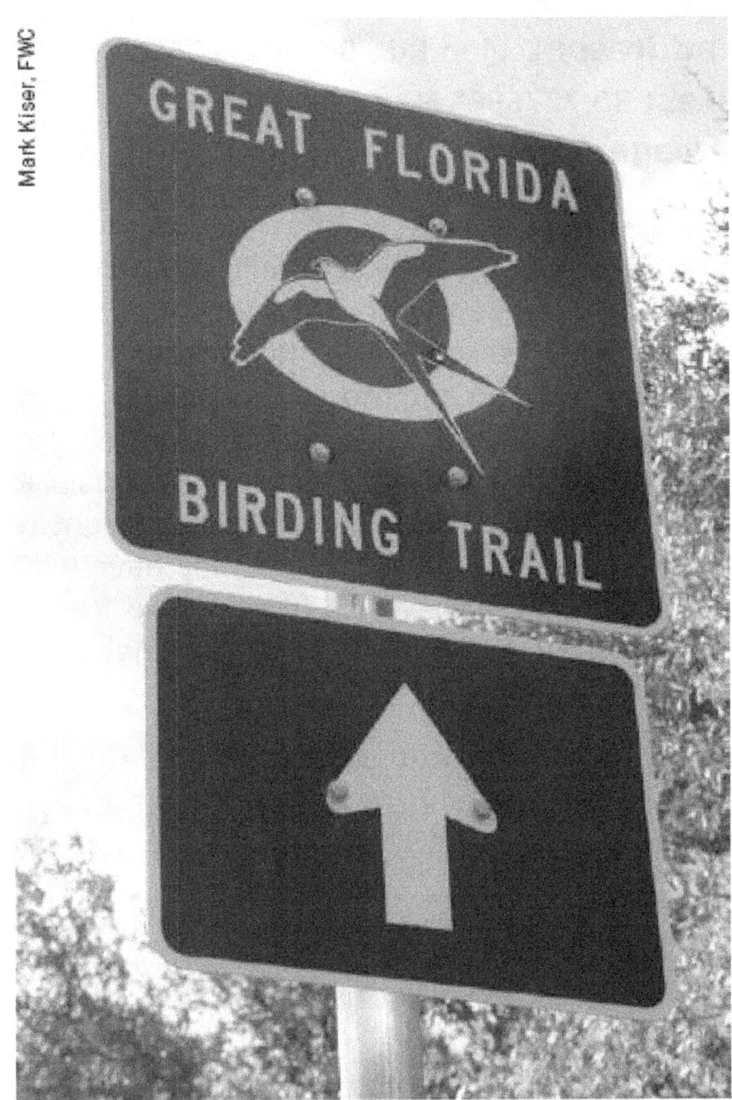

Road signs guide visitors to each destination in the Panhandle Section of the Great Florida Birding and Wildlife Trail.

58 Sneads Park

County: Jackson
Nearest city: Sneads
Physical address: Legion Rd., Sneads, 32460
Coordinates: 30.727696° N, -84.906788° W
Gazetteer page: 32
Size: 64 acres

This small waterfront park on Lake Seminole is worth a stop if you're in the area, to scope the open water for wintering ducks like Redheads, Canvasbacks, Lesser Scaup, Ring-necked Ducks, Buffehead, American Wigeon and more. Thousands of American Coots are often visible on the lake in winter; scan for Horned Grebes and Common Loons as well. Up for exploring? The park includes a boat ramp for access to the lake. Fields along the right (east) side of Legion Rd. north of the baseball diamonds may have wintering geese such as Canada, Snow, Greater White-fronted and Ross's. Check the roadside wires for American Kestrels; Western Kingbirds (rare) have also been sighted here.

Directions: From I-10, take exit 158 for CR 286. Head north for 5.2 mi. to US 90/SR 10 in Sneads. Turn right (east) and go 0.9 mi. Turn left (north) on Legion Rd. and drive 1.5 mi. to the parking area on the lake.

Open dawn to dusk. (850) 593-6636

J	F	M	A	M	J	J	A	S	O	N	D

Map K
Talquin Cluster

59 **Joe Budd Wildlife Management Area at Lake Talquin State Forest**

County: Gadsden

Nearest city: Midway

Physical address: Offce Rd. and Peters Rd., Midway, 32343

Coordinates: 30.509365° N, -84.538308° W (offce)

30.492610° N, -84.503975° W (Peters Rd. at Cattle Gap Rd.)

Gazetteer page: 33 and 49

Size: 11,039 acres

An extensive system of side roads closed to vehicles is open to exploration via foot, bicycle and equestrian traffc, and will yield wintering mixed focks of warblers, Wild Turkeys in the open felds and Northern Bobwhites in the pinewoods. After turning on Offce Rd., a large open pasture and dove feld on both sides of the road are good birding for wintering sparrows, Mourning Doves, Eastern Meadowlarks and American Kestrels and also serve some years as a display ground for courting American Woodcocks at dawn and dusk. Mississippi and Swallow-tailed Kites feed over pastures in spring/summer. Check edges of felds and woodlands for Blue Grosbeaks in summer as well. At the end of Offce Rd., a dike trail runs 0.7 miles one-way past sloughs good for warblers and Wood Ducks. Wood Storks are sometimes present at the Joe Budd Aquatic Education Center on Budd Pond, off Cattle Gap Rd.. The trail at the end of Plantation Rd. offers a vantage of Lake Talquin similar to High Bluff's (site # 60). Seasonal hunting takes place at this GFBWT site; please see Sharing Florida's public lands during hunting season for information on dates, regulations and more. The area is closed to other uses on hunt days. A WMA map is available from the website below.

Directions: From I-10 west of Tallahassee, take exit 192 onto US 90/SR 10 and head northwest. After 2.0 mi., turn left (southwest) towards Midway onto CR 268/MLK Blvd. Continue west for 6 mi. on CR 268/MLK Blvd. (changes to Highbridge Rd.), and turn left (south) on Offce Rd. to reach WMA headquarters. Other WMA roads can be accessed via Peters Rd. (See directions for site # 60; veer right onto Cattle Gap Rd. to access Joe Budd WMA).

Open dawn to dusk; closed on hunt days. (850) 717-8741
MyFWC.com/viewing/recreation/wmas/lead/joe-budd
www.freshfromforida.com/Divisions-Offces/Florida-Forest-Service

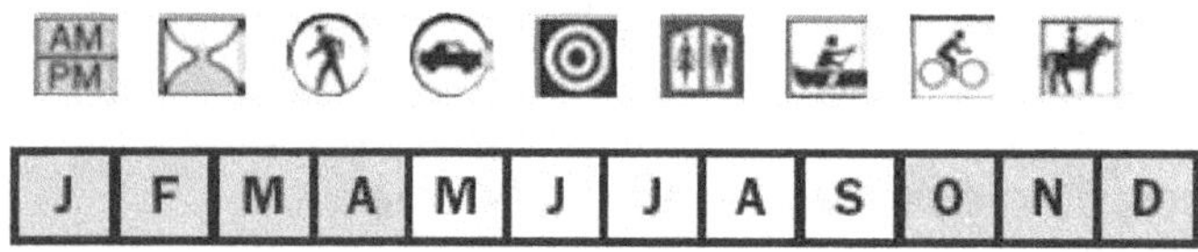

60 Lake Talquin State Forest: High Bluff Recreation Area

County: Gadsden

Nearest city: Midway

Physical address: High Bluff Landing Rd., Midway, 32343

Coordinates: 30.461752° N, -84.497412° W

Gazetteer page: 49 and 50

Size: 2 acres

Scan the lake from the fshing pier, looking for waders along the shoreline and in offshore trees, as well as wintering ducks on the open water, like Green-winged Teal and Lesser Scaup. Better yet, explore the lake from the water. Songbirds like Black-throated Blue Warblers and Northern and Louisiana Waterthrushes use the hardwoods lining the lake's edge in migration. Seasonal hunting takes place at this GFBWT site; please see Sharing Florida's public lands during hunting season for information on dates, regulations and more.

Directions: From I-10 west of Tallahassee, take exit 192 for US 90/SR 10 and head northwest. After 2.0 mi., turn left (southwest) towards Midway onto CR 268/MLK Blvd. Go 2.4 mi. on CR 268/MLK Blvd. to Peters Rd. and turn left (west). Drive 1.1 mi. and turn left (south) onto High Bluff Landing Rd., which dead ends at the site after 2.6 mi.

Open dawn to dusk. (850) 681-5963
www.freshfromforida.com/Divisions-Offces/Florida-Forest-Service

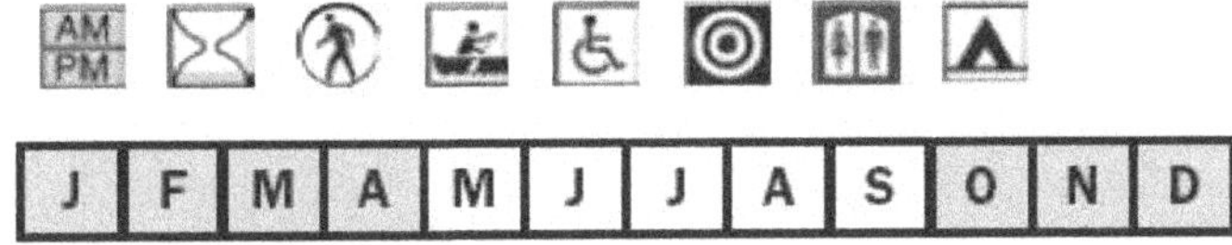

An eloquent songster, the Wood Thrush is a breeding bird of the Panhandle and extreme North Florida. It feeds mainly on insects.

61 Lake Talquin State Forest: Bear Creek Educational Forest

County: Gadsden

Nearest city: Quincy

Physical address: 8125 Pat Thomas Pkwy., Quincy, 32351

Coordinates: 30.478155° N, -84.626724° W

Gazetteer page: 49

Size: 492 acres

The entrance trail to this site is a paved interpretive trail, which then connects to the 2.5-mile Ravine Trail and the 3.0-mile Bear Creek Trail. The former hugs the creek ravine, and its hardwood forest is good for migrants like Wood Thrushes and Veeries. The pine fatwoods of the longer Bear Creek Trail are good for Northern Bobwhites and Wild Turkeys. Take water and insect repellent, and pick up a map at the entrance kiosk. This site offers something for people of all birding skill and mobility levels. Butterfy viewing here is best in spring. Check fowering trees, especially along the Ravine Trail, for gossamer-wing butterfies such as Henry's Elfn, Banded Hairstreak and Spring and Summer Azures.

Directions: From I-10 south of Quincy, take exit 181 for SR 267/Pat Thomas Pkwy. Drive south for 4.3 mi. and cross CR 65B; the entrance is 0.4 mi. further south on the left (east) side of the road.

Open dawn to dusk. (850) 681-5963
www.freshfromforida.com/Divisions-Offces/Florida-Forest-Service

The Eastern Tiger Swallowtail is a large, familiar butterfy found throughout most of Florida. Males are yellow, but females can be either black or yellow. The caterpillars feed on trees such as red maple, wild cherry, sweetbay and tulip tree. Look for adults feeding on thistle, ironweed and milkweed in meadows, parks and roadsides.

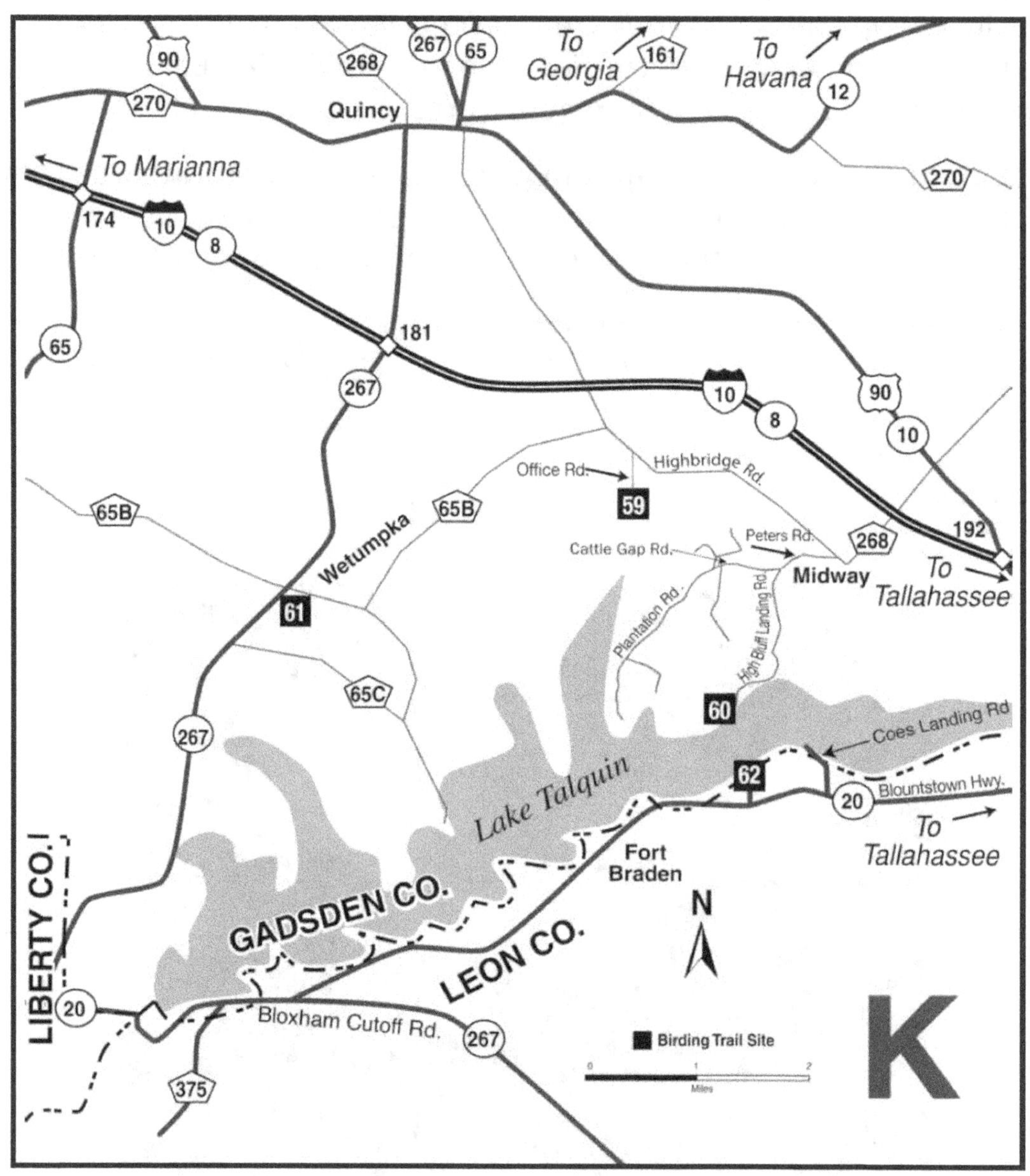

Northern Bobwhite

62	**Lake Talquin State Forest: Fort Braden Trails**

County: Leon
Nearest city: Tallahassee

Physical address: SR 20/Blountstown Hwy., Tallahassee, 32310
Coordinates: 30.438199° N, -84.495804° W
Gazetteer page: 49 and 50
Size: 1,242 acres

This site offers extensive hiking trails that are blazed in orange (compared to horse trails in pink or yellow). Pick up a map at the entrance and bring water. One of the best trail choices is the Center Loop: hike north from the parking area and stay right at every split on the orange-blazed trail to make a 2-mile loop back to the parking area. The trail will take you through open areas and xeric oak uplands good for Wild Turkeys and White-eyed Vireos, then reach bluffs overlooking Lake Talquin. It follows the lake edge for nearly a mile before circling back through the uplands. Watch overhead for raptors and scan the lake for wintering ducks and wading birds. Weedy and brushy areas have wintering sparrows including Chipping, Song and White-throated.

Directions: From the intersection of SR 263/Capital Circle and SR 20/Blountstown Hwy. in Tallahassee, take SR 20 west for 8.7 mi.; the trailhead parking area is on the right (north) side of the road.

Open dawn to dusk. (850) 681-5963
www.freshfromforida.com/Divisions-Offces/Florida-Forest-Service

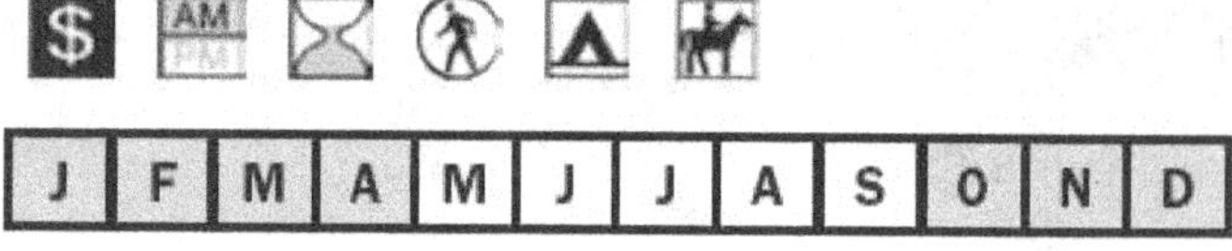

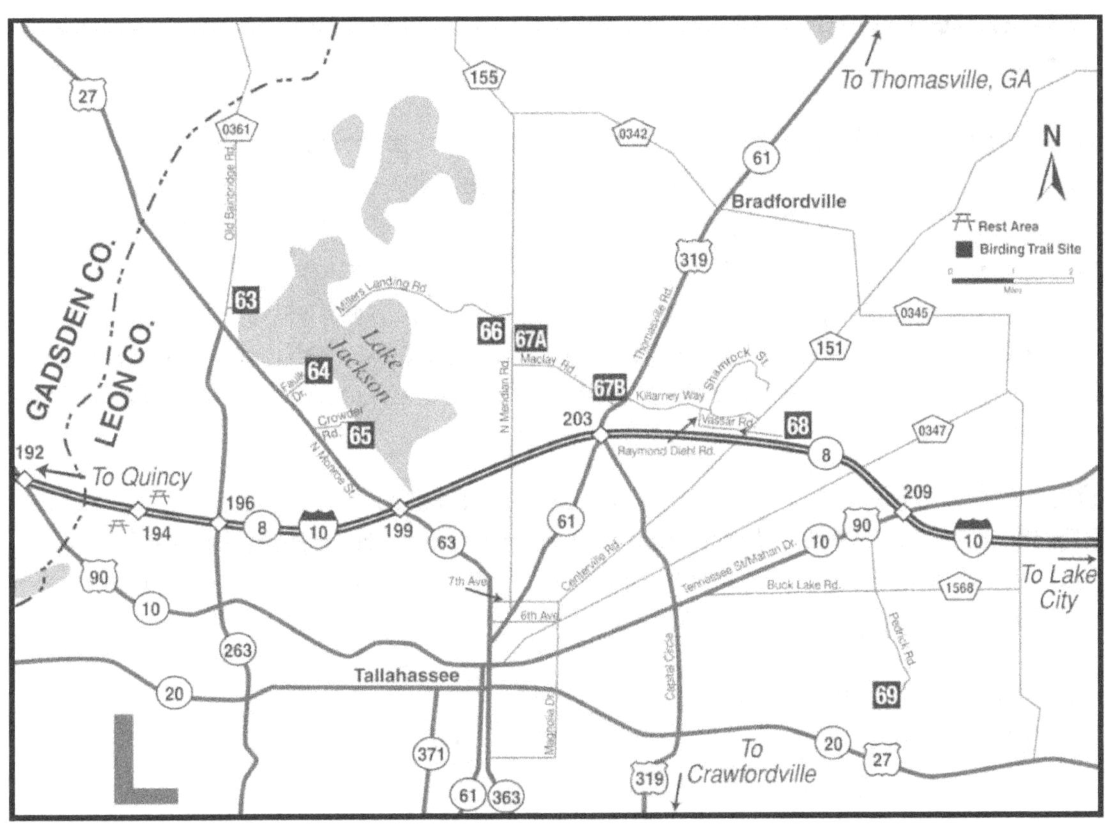

Map L
White-breasted Nuthatch Cluster

63 | **J. Lee Vause Park**

County: Leon

Nearest city: Tallahassee
Physical address: 6024 Old Bainbridge Rd., Tallahassee, 32303
Coordinates: 30.537105° N, -84.361323° W
Gazetteer page: 34
Size: 26 acres

This small park has a well-developed center, but down by the lake its sunny, woody edges are a haven for birds like Orange-crowned Warblers and the occasional Yellow-breasted Chat. A boardwalk and pier provide a view of Lake Jackson, where you can look for a diversity of wading birds like Wood Storks as well as wintering ducks and coots. Don't forget fyovers by Ospreys and Bald Eagles, as well as breeding Red-shouldered, Red-tailed and Broad-winged Hawks in spring and summer!

Directions: From I-10 in Tallahassee, take exit 199 for US 27/N. Monroe St. Drive north for 4.6 mi. and turn right (north) on CR 0361/Old Bainbridge Rd.; the park is 0.3 mi. ahead on the right (east) side of the road.

Open dawn to dusk. (850) 606-1470
www.leoncountyf.gov/parks/park_index.asp

J	F	M	A	M	J	J	A	S	O	N	D

64 Faulk Drive Landing

County: Leon
Nearest city: Tallahassee
Physical address: Faulk Dr., Tallahassee, 32303

Coordinates: 30.521403° N, -84.324292° W

Gazetteer page: 34

Size: 0.2 acres

Another access to Lake Jackson, this one is a little more rustic, and your tires (not to mention your feet!) may get muddy at times of higher water. It's best to park back from the landing and walk in, watching fence posts and small oaks for fycatchers and warblers. At the landing, scan for egrets, herons, White Ibises and waterfowl; Black-bellied Whistling-Ducks have turned up here, as have Roseate Spoonbills. The grassy area to the south of the landing may have Common Ground-Doves, Eastern Bluebirds and Common Yellowthroats, plus sparrows (such as Swamp and Savannah) in winter. Launch a canoe or kayak here to explore Lake Jackson in more detail. Worth a stop if you're in the area. Seasonal hunting takes place at this GFBWT site; please see Sharing Florida's public lands during hunting season for information on dates, regulations and more.

Directions: From I-10 in Tallahassee, take exit 199 for US 27/N. Monroe St. Drive north for 2.7 mi. and turn right (northeast) on Faulk Dr.; the site is 1.4 mi. ahead at the end of the road.

Open dawn to dusk. (850) 606-1470
www.leoncountyf.gov/parks/park_index.asp

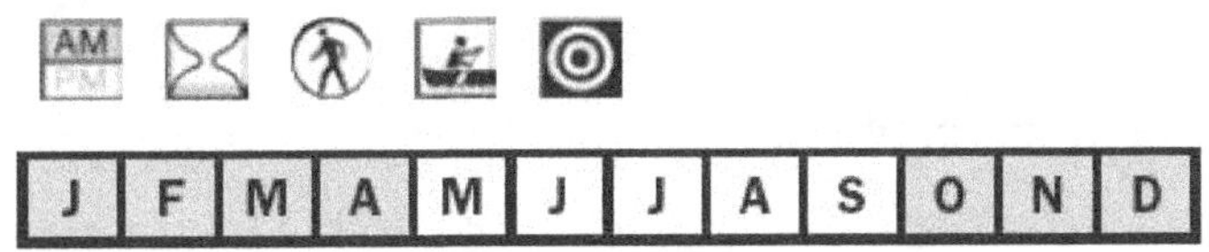

65 Crowder Landing

County: Leon

Nearest city: Tallahassee
Physical address: Crowder Rd., Tallahassee, 32303
Coordinates: 30.507436° N, -84.313444° W
Gazetteer page: 34
Size: 0.6 acres

This small boat landing warrants a quick stop if you're in the area, because it provides another vantage of Lake Jackson. Wintering ducks and coots are plentiful on the lake in winter, as are wading birds like Snowy Egrets and Little Blue Herons. Sandhill Cranes appear on occasion and in 2002 a Hudsonian Godwit was discovered here! Lake Jackson is known for its tendency to disappear down a sinkhole in its middle at times of low water; to birders, it's known for less common fycatchers (Vermillion, for example), and songbirds in migration. When it's hot, it's hot. When it's not...

Directions: From I-10 in Tallahassee, take exit 199 for US 27/N. Monroe St. Drive north for 1.7 mi. and turn right (east) on Crowder Rd. Follow Crowder Rd. for 1.2 mi. as it bends north, then east; the site is at the end, on the lake.

Open dawn to dusk. (850) 606-1470
www.leoncountyf.gov/parks/park_index.asp

J	F	M	A	M	J	J	A	S	O	N	D

<table><tr><td>66</td><td>Elinor Klapp-Phipps Park</td></tr></table>

County: Leon
Nearest city: Tallahassee

Physical address: 701 Miller Landing Rd., Tallahassee, 32312
Coordinates: 30.536493° N, -84.280792° W
Gazetteer page: 34
Size: 670 acres

Elinor Klapp-Phipps Park on Lake Jackson has areas of longleaf pine restoration, but its real asset is the beautiful deciduous slope forest following the trickle of small streams down to the big lake. Eastern Bluebirds, Indigo Buntings and Wild Turkeys use open grassy areas along the powerline entrance and horse trailer entrance. As the trails dive into the hammock, start watching and listening for migrants like Wood and Gray-cheeked Thrushes and Blackburnian Warblers. Down by the large bat house on Lake Victoria at stop # 17, scope for Anhingas, Tricolored Herons, and Ospreys; Black-bellied Whistling-Ducks have bred here recently. The Lake Jackson area is known for unusual sightings, like occasional wintering Western Tanagers, so bird with an open mind! Butterfy viewing is also quite good at this park, spring through fall. Unlike many sites, mid-summer has an impressive variety of butterfy species; look for spread-winged skippers, including Silver-spotted, Golden-banded, Hoary Edge and Southern Cloudywing along the woodland trails and in the open meadows. Trails at this park are extensive and winding. Pick up a trail map and butterfy checklist at the entrance (or download them from the website below) and pay attention to your chosen route.

Reinhard Geisler

Directions: From I-10 in Tallahassee, take exit 203 for US 319/SR 61/Thomasville Rd. Drive north for 0.9 mi. and turn left (west) on Maclay Rd. Follow Maclay Rd. for 2.2 mi. to its end and turn right (north) on N. Meridian Rd. Drive 1.0 mi. and turn left (west) on Miller's Landing Rd.; the park entrance is 0.2 mi. ahead on the left (south) side of the road. Additional entrances (gates A and B) are located further west at 1275 and 1775 Miller Landing Rd.

Open dawn to dusk. (850) 891-3866, (850) 891-3975 www.talgov.com

 **67 Alfred B. Maclay Gardens State Park**

County: Leon

Nearest city: Tallahassee

Physical address: 3540 Thomasville Rd., Tallahassee, 32309

Coordinates: 30.534672° N, -84.277454° W (Lake Overstreet) 30.513532° N, -84.247467° W (main entrance)

Gazetteer page: 34

Size: 1,179 acres

More widely known for its manicured gardens, this park also offers native habitat that is better for birdwatching. Try the brief trails along the lake at the Lake Hall Recreation Area for wintering Orange-crowned Warblers and Blue-headed Vireos. A few Dark-eyed Juncos make an appearance here in winter; Brown Creepers and Winter

Wrens may also be present. Check the lakes for wintering ducks and then for drinking Purple Martins beginning in February. For a longer hike, hit the Lake Overstreet multi-use trails (5 miles worth) off Meridian Road. These are more rustic so be sure to pick up a map and bring water. Birds like Red-headed Woodpeckers, Brown-headed and White-breasted Nuthatches, Great Horned Owls and Chuck-wills-widows can all be found here. The recreation area and gardens have wheelchair access. Loaner optics are available.

Directions: (A) Lake Overstreet Trailhead: From the intersection of Meridian and Maclay roads, drive north on Meridian 0.9 mi., turn left (west) and enter the parking lot for Forest Meadows Park & Athletic Center; the trailhead is directly across the street on the east side of Meridian. (B) Main entrance: From I-10 in Tallahassee, take exit 203 for US 319/SR 61/Thomasville Rd. Drive north for 0.9 mi. and turn left (west) on Maclay Rd. The park entrance is 0.2 mi. on the right (north) side of the road.

Open year round, 8 AM to sundown. (850) 487-4556
www.foridastateparks.org/maclaygardens

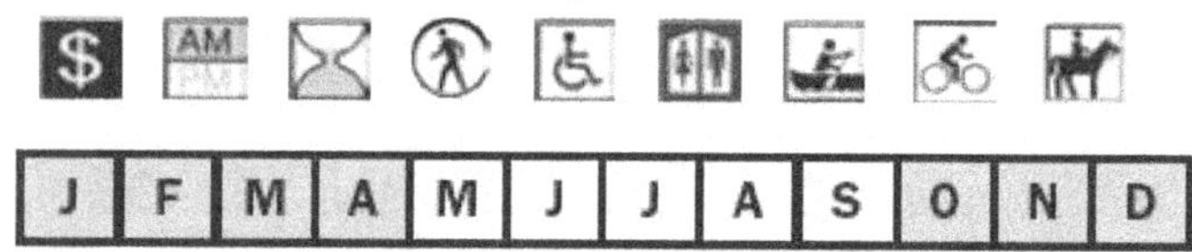

68 A. J. Henry Park

County: Leon
Nearest city: Tallahassee
Physical address: 3000 A. J. Henry Park Dr., Tallahassee, 32309
Coordinates: 30.507040° N, -84.217947° W (north entrance)
30.503435° N, -84.218606° W (south entrance)

Gazetteer page: 34 and 50

Size: 72 acres

A. J. Henry Park is a small city property with some nice topography and habitats, including hardwood forest-covered slopes which descend down to a lake. Accordingly, this park attracts fallouts of migrants like Veery, Ovenbird and Magnolia Warbler, among others. Raptors like Mississippi Kite and Broad-winged Hawk hunt for prey here in late spring and summer, and Blue-winged Teal, Ring-necked Duck and the occasional Redhead or Common Goldeneye can be found on the lake in winter. The area surrounding the lake and the lower (north) parking area offer the most productive birding. Extensive trails at the upper (south) parking area are appealing, but the thicker understory can make it hard to spot birds, frustrating those who don't know bird calls and songs.

Directions: From I-10 in Tallahassee, take exit 203 for US 319/SR 61/Thomasville Rd. Drive north for 0.9 mi. to Killarney Way and turn right (southeast). There are two approaches to the site off of this road. For the south entrance, proceed east on Killarney Way and turn right (south) onto Raymond Diehl Rd., then turn left (east) on Vassar Rd. Take Vassar Rd. to its end and turn right (south) on Whitney Dr. The park is 150 yds. on the left (east) side of the road. For the north entrance, follow Killarney Way to the end and turn right (southeast) on Shamrock St. After 0.3 mi., turn right (south) on Gardenview Way and right (southwest) again after 0.3 mi. onto A. J. Henry Park Dr. The entrance is 0.2 mi. ahead.

Open 8 AM to dusk. (850) 891-3866
www.talgov.com

Common Goldeneye

Rusty Blackbird

69 J. R. Alford Greenway

County: Leon

Nearest city: Tallahassee

Physical address: 2500 S. Pedrick Rd., Tallahassee, 32317

Coordinates: 30.444486° N, -84.175759° W
Gazetteer page: 50
Size: 874 acres

This greenway is a collection of old pastures and woodlands now used for passive recreation. Seventeen miles of multi-use trails invite many hours of exploration. From the parking area follow the trail due east across the frst pasture (watch for Purple Martins and Eastern Bluebirds around the gourds and nest boxes) and veer either way at the fork to continue through a series of open felds. Watch overhead for Red-tailed Hawks; mixed focks of wintering Palm Warblers and White-throated Sparrows fit in the weedy edges. Pastures are managed for a mosaic of early succession habitats; wintering Grasshopper Sparrows skulk in the grass (when it's left high) as do Eastern Meadowlarks. American Kestrels, Eastern Phoebes and Loggerhead Shrikes stand lookout on snags and Wood Storks and Double-crested Cormorants can be seen fying overhead to Lake Lafayette at sunset. From the parking lot, another trail leads to the south and winds east through hardwoods good for Red-shouldered and Cooper's Hawks. Download a map and pay attention to your route. Trails can be confusing at times; a GPS unit is quite useful here. Consider biking this property to cover more ground.

Directions: From the intersection of US 319/Capital Circle and US 90/Tennessee St./Mahan Dr. in Tallahassee, drive 0.7 mi. east on US 90 and turn right (east) on Buck Lake Rd. After 2.0 mi., turn right (south) onto Pedrick Rd.; the entrance and parking are 1.6 mi. ahead at the end of the road.

Open dawn to dusk. (850) 606-1470
cms.leoncountyf.gov

<table>
<tr><td>J</td><td>F</td><td>M</td><td>A</td><td>M</td><td>J</td><td>J</td><td>A</td><td>S</td><td>O</td><td>N</td><td>D</td></tr>
</table>

Map M
Mississippi Kite Cluster

70 | **Apalachicola National Forest: Leon Sinks Geological Area**

County: Leon

Nearest city: Woodville

Physical address: US 319/Crawfordville Hwy., Tallahassee, 32305

Coordinates: 30.306785° N, -84.345082° W

Gazetteer page: 50

Size: 640 acres

This recreation area in the east portion of the Apalachicola National Forest is different from the lower, longleaf savannah habitats of the tracts closer to the river. Here, higher sandhills of pine and turkey oak are broken by erosion in the underlying limestone, causing deep, dramatic crystal blue sinkholes which are rimmed with hardwoods. Upon entering the hiking trail, turn left at the T-junction for the shorter trail (1.7 miles) and return on the short-cut (0.5 mile) through a tupelo swamp. Listen for Barred Owls, Northern Parulas and Prothonotary Warblers near the wetlands, and watch for Blue-headed Vireos and Carolina Chickadees in the pinewoods. By turning right at the T-junction, you'll choose the longer 2.5-mile loop past a series of large sinkholes. Watch for Wild Turkeys, Hermit Thrushes and White-eyed Vireos in the sandhills, as well as songbirds like Yellow-billed Cuckoos in hardwoods sloping into the sinks. In spring, wild azaleas along the Gum Swamp Trail attract many swallowtail butterfies. Little Wood-Satyr and Red-spotted Purple can occur in any wooded stretch. Near the sinkholes, look for Golden-banded Skippers. Bring water and sunscreen.

Directions: From the intersection of US 319/SR 263/Capital Circle SW and US 319/SR 369/SR 61/Crawfordville Rd. in Tallahassee, drive south on Crawfordville Rd. for 5.8 mi.; the site is on the right (west) side of the road.

Open year round, 8 AM to 8 PM. (850) 926-3561
www.fs.usda.gov/apalachicola

J	F	M	A	M	J	J	A	S	O	N	D

One of the most famous and recognizable butterfies in North America, the Monarch undertakes an extensive migration each fall to hibernation sites in California and Mexico. Large numbers gather on the Gulf Coast in October at locations like St. Marks National Wildlife Refuge in Wakulla County. A festival held at the refuge each year coincides with the Monarch's migration. Milkweeds are important plants for both caterpillars and adults.

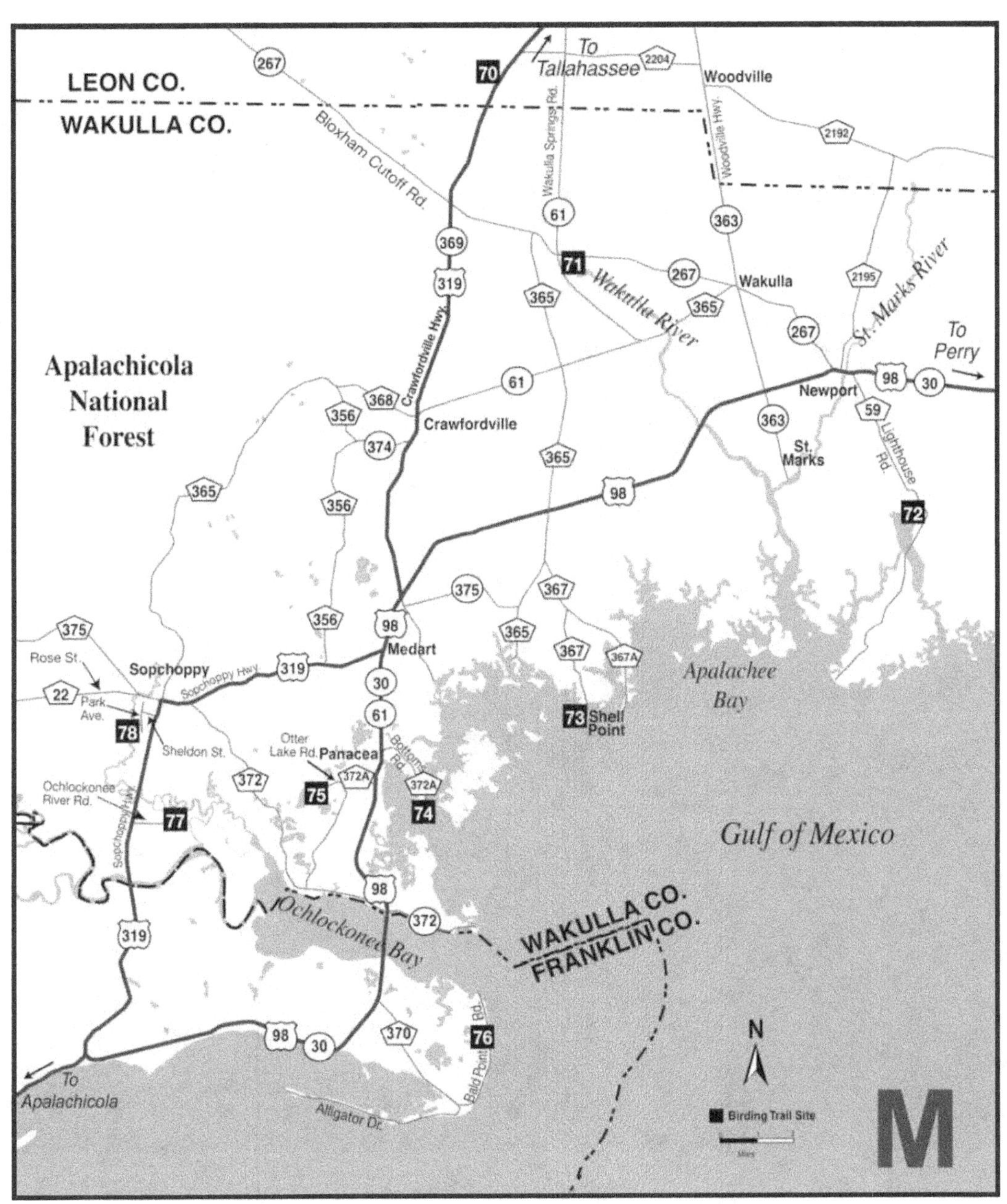

LEON CO.
WAKULLA CO.
267
70
To Tallahassee
2204
Woodville
Bloxham Cutoff Rd.
Wakulla Springs Rd.
Woodville Hwy.
2192
61
363
369
71
2195
319
267
Wakulla
365
St. Marks River
365
Apalachicola
National
Forest
365
Crawfordville Hwy.
368
267
To
Perry
356
61
Newport
98
30
374
Crawfordville
365
363
59
Lighthouse Rd.
St.
Marks
365
98
72
375
367
98
356
375
365
367
Apalachee
Bay
375
Medart
367
367A
Rose St.
Sopchoppy
319
30
73 Shell
Point
22
Park Ave.
Sopchoppy Hwy.
61
78
Otter
Lake Rd. Panacea
Bottoms Rd.
Gulf of Mexico
Sheldon St.
372
372A
Ochlockonee
River Rd.
372
75
372A
74
77
Sopchoppy Hwy.
98
Ochlockonee Bay
WAKULLA CO.
FRANKLIN CO.
372
319
Bald Point Rd.
98
30
370
76
N
To
Apalachicola
Alligator Dr.
Birding Trail Site
Miles
M

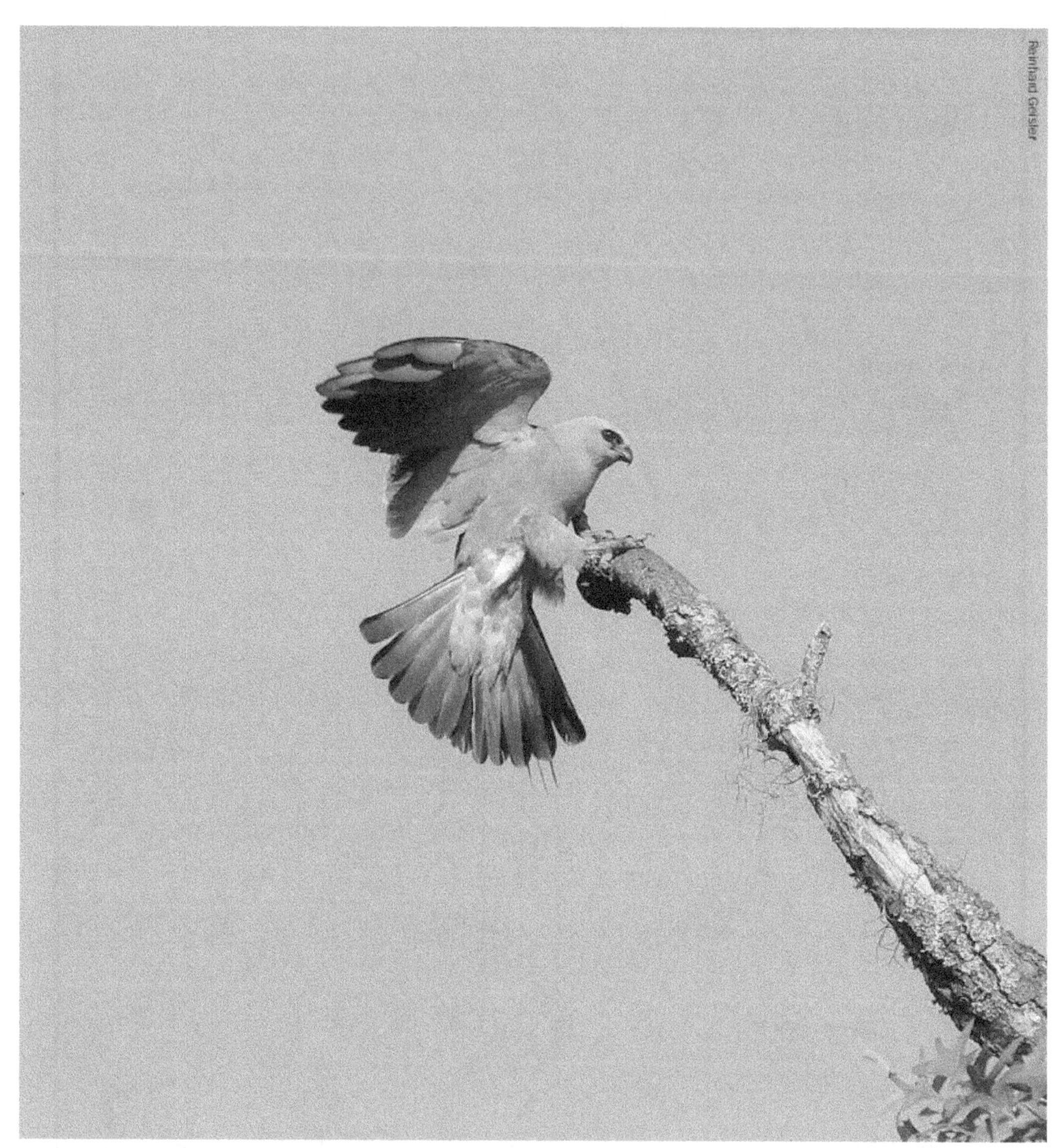

Mississippi Kite

71 **Edward Ball Wakulla Springs State Park**

County: Wakulla
Nearest city: Wakulla Springs
Physical address: 550 Wakulla Park Dr., Wakulla Springs, 32327
Coordinates: 30.243337° N, -84.310614° W
Gazetteer page: 50
Size: 6,055 acres

Hiking trails throughout this park provide access to foodplain forest good for Summer Tanagers and Ovenbirds in migration and Great Crested Flycatchers and Northern Parulas in summer. The primary attraction, however, is the access to Wakulla's first magnitude spring. From the pier, look for Anhingas, Common Gallinules, Pied-billed Grebes and wintering Hooded Mergansers, as well as roosting Black Vultures in the cypress. Better yet, take one of the park's river cruises to get excellent views of the aforementioned plus Least Bitterns, Yellow-crowned Night-Herons, Barred Owls and White Ibises. Alligators, Suwannee River Cooters and mullet are commonly seen; manatees are sometimes found in the river and spring as well. In years past this park was known for Limpkins, but today they are almost never seen here. However, the park staff is reintroducing native apple snails, the Limpkin's main prey item, to entice Limpkins to return. The spectacular, 1930s-era lodge has roosting Chimney Swifts in summer. Butterfy viewing is best here in late spring and fall. Many swallowtail and hairstreak species are seen on fowering trees and shrubs in spring. Texan Crescents and Appalachian Browns are regularly seen on the hiking trails north of the Wakulla River. The park hosts an extensive wildlife and birding festival each spring.

Directions: From the intersection of SR 263/Capital Circle SW and US 319/SR 369/SR 61/Crawfordville Rd. in Tallahassee, drive south on Crawfordville Rd. for 2.1 mi. Take a slight left to stay on SR 61/Wakulla Springs Rd. and go 7.4 mi. Turn left (east) on SR

267/Bloxham Cutoff Rd.; the site is 0.1 mi. ahead on the right (south) side of the road.

Open year round, 8 AM to sundown. (850) 561-7276
www.foridastateparks.org/wakullasprings

 **St. Marks National Wildlife Refuge: St. Marks Unit (Headquarters)**
*Gateway**

County: Wakulla/Jefferson
Nearest city: St. Marks
Physical address: 1255 Lighthouse Rd., Crawfordville, 32327
Coordinates: 30.159923° N, -84.153055° W
Gazetteer page: 50 and 51
Size: 29,529 acres

Spanning three counties, and with more than 300 recorded bird species, the 68,000-acre St. Marks NWR is a must-see. The St. Marks Unit includes refuge headquarters and the historic St. Marks Lighthouse; it's also the unit most popular with birders and wildlife viewers, for good reason. Stop briefy at the visitor center for a map and to check the sightings log. A pond and trail here can be good for White-throated Sparrows, Pileated Woodpeckers, Belted Kingfishers, Eastern Phoebes and more, but other trails are more rewarding. From north to south along the main road: the helicopter pad accessed from the primitive hiking trails is good for wintering sparrows such as Henslow's; East River Pool can be good for waterfowl in winter; Stoney Bayou Pool and the Mounds Pools hold shovelers, coots and the spectrum of wading birds in winter, and the trail around Mounds Pool # 3 is particularly good for Northern Pintails and Snow Geese in winter. Stoney Bayou Pool # 2 and Mounds Pool # 3 are also good places to look for American Black Ducks. The Headquarters Pond viewing platform offers the occasional Sora and Purple Gallinule, as well as wintering teal and year-round waders. The Mounds Trail around Tower Pond is very good for migrant songbirds like Yellow-billed Cuckoos and Indigo Buntings, as well as Brown-headed Nuthatches in the pines and ducks and shorebirds in the pond. At the road's terminus at the lighthouse, look for common wintering waterfowl plus Redheads, Canvasbacks, Nelson's Sparrows, shorebirds and more. Scaup, Buffehead, Horned Grebes, and Common and Red-throated Loons winter in the Gulf, and Least Bitterns, Seaside Sparrows, shorebirds and Clapper Rails breed in the marshes. Oystercatchers, pelicans and gulls loaf on pilings and offshore oyster bars. Butterfy viewing is best here in fall, especially September and October. Monarch butterfies congregate here along Apalachee Bay on their fall migration to Mexico; a Monarch festival is held each October to celebrate this phenomenon. Hundreds of Monarchs may be seen on a mid-October day. Along Lighthouse Dr., keep your eyes open for Gulf Fritillaries and Long-tailed Skippers, plus American Alligators, Bobcats, Northern River Otters, and Florida Black Bears. Though you may not see one just yet, a Whooping Crane reintroduction project began in 2009. Bring water, food, sun protection and bug spray.

Directions: From the intersection of US 98/SR 30 and SR 363/Woodville Hwy. north of the town of St. Marks, drive east on US 98 approx. 2.5 mi. and turn right (south) on CR 59/Lighthouse Rd., just east of the St. Marks River Bridge. The refuge entrance is 3.0 mi. ahead; the visitor center is 0.6 mi. farther south on the right.

Open dawn to dusk. (850) 925-6121
www.fws.gov/saintmarks

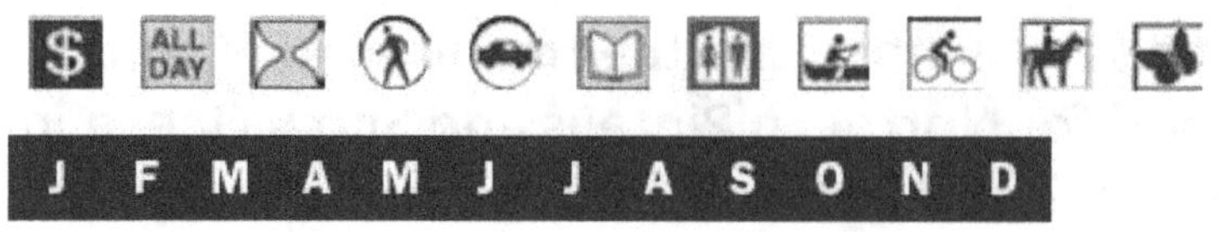

*see **"Gateways"** section for more information._

73 | Shell Point Beach Park

County: Wakulla
Nearest city: Crawfordville
Physical address: 117 Beaty Taff Dr., Crawfordville, 32327
Coordinates: 30.058004° N, -84.290519° W
Gazetteer page: 50

This Wakulla County park is worth a quick stop for a picnic lunch and a look for shorebirds. The parking area offers an easy vantage of loafing shorebirds in fall-winter-spring such as Short-billed Dowitchers, Dunlin, Willets, Marbled Godwits, Black Skimmers and more. Keep an eye peeled for the occasional migrating Peregrine Falcon watching the shorebirds even more closely than you! Summer is busy with swimming/boating visitors. Shorebirds are more diverse and plentiful in cool weather months.

Directions: From the intersection of US 98/SR 30 and SR 363/Woodville Hwy. north of St. Marks, drive west on US 98 approx. 8.0 mi. and turn left (south) on CR 365/Spring Creek Hwy. Turn left after 2.0 mi. onto CR 367/Shell Point Rd. Continue approx. 5 mi. on CR 367 (do not take CR 367A at the fork) and turn left (southeast) on Beaty Taff Dr. Go 0.2 mi. to the parking area on the right (south) side of the road.

Open dawn to dusk. (850) 926-7227
www.wcprd.com

74 Bottoms Road Boat Ramp

County: Wakulla

Nearest city: Panacea

Physical address: Bottoms Rd., Panacea, 32346

Coordinates: 30.016052° N, -84.368326° W

Gazetteer page: 50

Bottoms Road extends out through salt marsh to a county-owned boat launch on the Gulf. Along the way, watch and listen for Clapper Rails, Virginia Rails (winter) and wading birds in the marsh, plus Northern Harriers cruising the fats in winter. The marsh is also a good place to look for Nelson's Sparrow (winter) and Seaside Sparrow (year-round). From the shoulder along the road, scope the offshore sandbars for loafing terns, gulls and shorebirds. The large, dirt pull-off on the east side of the road (0.5 miles north of the boat ramp) is private property. The marsh is locally known for occasional Short-eared Owl sightings in winter, so watch for these daytime hunters gliding low over the marsh like Northern Harriers or perched on low posts amidst the rushes. From the boat ramp, scan the waters for ducks and scoters.

Directions: From the intersection of US 98/SR 30 and SR 363/Woodville Hwy. north of the town of St. Marks, drive west on US 98 for 16.6 mi. and turn left (east) on CR 372A/Bottoms Rd. just before the town of Panacea. Park along the shoulder (where safe) and at the boat ramp (2.6 mi. ahead) at the end of the road.

Open dawn to dusk.

75 St. Marks National Wildlife Refuge: Otter Lake Recreation Area

County: Wakulla

Nearest city: Panacea

Physical address: Otter Lake Rd., Panacea, 32346

Coordinates: 30.026031° N, -84.416565° W

Gazetteer page: 50

Size: 11,387 acres

Though not as famous as the St. Marks Unit, St. Marks NWR's Panacea Unit offers good birding too. Make a quick trip to the picnic area and boat launch at the end to check the cypress for Prothonotary Warblers and occasional wading birds, or choose to hike one of the longer trails: the south Piney Ridge Trail loop (5 miles) or the north Otter Lake Trail loop (9 miles). The latter runs through pinewoods interrupted by occasional bayheads and wetlands. Watch for Red-headed and Red-cockaded Woodpeckers, Wild Turkeys and Northern Bobwhites. At dusk, check the boat launch for Wood Storks, egrets and both vultures coming to roost; Ospreys nest in the area. Swallow-tailed Kites can be seen soaring overhead in spring and summer. There is some hunting along the hiking trails so check the trailhead signs before entering and carry water and sunscreen with you. See Sharing Florida's public lands during hunting season for more information.

Directions: From the intersection of US 98/SR 30 and SR 363/Woodville Hwy. north of the town of St. Marks, drive west on US

98 for 17.5 mi. and turn right (west) on CR 372A/Otter Lake Rd. The site is at the west end of Otter Lake Rd.

Open dawn to dusk. (850) 925-6121
www.fws.gov/saintmarks

| 76 | **Bald Point State Park** |

County: Franklin
Nearest city: Alligator Point
Physical address: Bald Point Rd., Alligator Point, 32346
Coordinates: 29.937605° N, -84.337327° W (main entrance)
29.914581° N, -84.336804° W (Sunrise Beach access)
Gazetteer page: 61 inset
Size: 4,859 acres

Located on the south side of Ochlockonee Bay, this state park offers great birding and wildlife viewing. Its geography and location provide a prime vantage of the raptor migration in October, as Peregrine Falcons, Northern Harriers and others cruise down the beach. Overwintering shorebirds like Black-bellied Plovers and Dunlin use the beach and estuary, and when horseshoe crabs are spawning (which can be impressive), large numbers of shorebirds gather to feast on the crabs' eggs. A few sea turtles also nest here in summer. In spring, migratory songbirds like Black-throated Green Warblers and Indigo Buntings make landfall in the park's hammocks; live oaks surrounding the upper parking area can be quite good. Year-round, listen for raucous Clapper Rails and Marsh Wrens from the observation boardwalk, which overlooks pristine marshes near the upper parking lot. Groove-billed Anis are rare winter visitors. An extensive hiking trail network begins 1.6 miles south of the main entrance gate, on the west side of the road, across from the Sunrise Beach access. These foot trails wind through mesic, wet and scrubby fatwoods (home to Brown-headed Nuthatches) and around freshwater marshes, swamps and ponds, which have wading birds and ducks when water levels are favorable. The park is also a staging point for Monarch butterfies on their fall trans-Gulf migration. Large numbers of several other species concentrate here in fall as well, including Gulf Fritillary, Common Buckeye, Long-tailed Skipper and Ocola Skipper. In early spring, Eastern Pygmy Blues can be abundant in the salt marsh. Ceraunus Blues can be common in fall. Guided tours are available for groups; call 2 weeks in advance. Fishing and sunbathing are popular in nice weather.

Directions: From Panacea, drive west (head south) on US 98/SR 30 for 7 mi. and turn left (southeast) on CR 370/Alligator Dr. Drive 3.8 mi. and turn left (east) on Bald Point Rd.; the main entrance gate is 2.8 mi. ahead. Sunrise Beach and trailhead access are 1.2 mi. north of the intersection with Alligator Dr.

Open year round, 8 AM to sundown. (850) 349-9146
www.foridastateparks.org/baldpoint

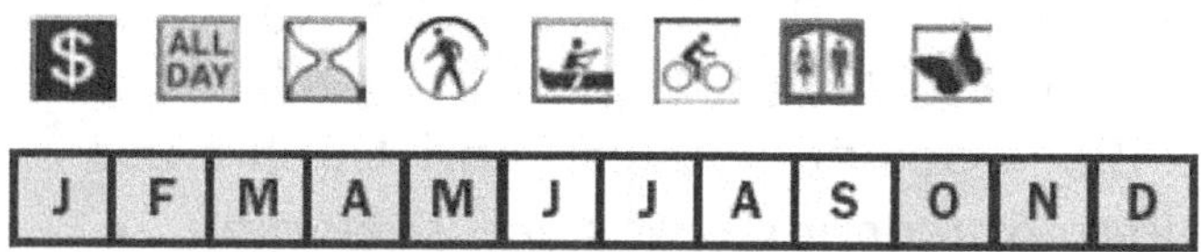

77 Ochlockonee River State Park

County: Wakulla
Nearest city: Sopchoppy

Physical address: 429 State Park Rd., Sopchoppy, 32358
Coordinates: 29.998902° N, -84.485259° W
Gazetteer page: 50 and 61 inset
Size: 543 acres

Upon entering this state park, ask at the gate for the locations of active Red-cockaded Woodpecker (RCWs) cavities or recent sightings. Head to the parking area at the end of the road, and in the northeastern corner, take the "Scenic Drive" loop road, which you may drive, bike or walk. Watch and listen for RCWs, Pine Warblers, Eastern Towhees and Common Yellowthroats. You may also hike the Pine Flatwoods Trail, which originates at the same parking lot. This park is well-known for its "snow white" Eastern Gray Squirrels (no, they are not albinos). If you choose to launch a canoe here, ask at the gate about water levels and clearance. Prothonotary Warblers and Wood Storks may be seen along the river, as well as skulking Green Herons, Limpkins and Least Bitterns in the brushy margins. For early morning access, consider camping overnight, and enjoy the sounds of Chuck-wills-widows and Eastern Screech-Owls after dark.

Snowy Plover

Directions: From the intersection of Rose St. and US 319/SR 377/Sopchoppy Hwy. in Sopchoppy, head south on Sopchoppy Hwy. for 4.4 mi. Turn left (east) on Ochlockonee River Rd.; the entrance is 1.2 mi. ahead.

Open year round, 8 AM to sundown. (850) 962-2771
www.foridastateparks.org/ochlockoneeriver

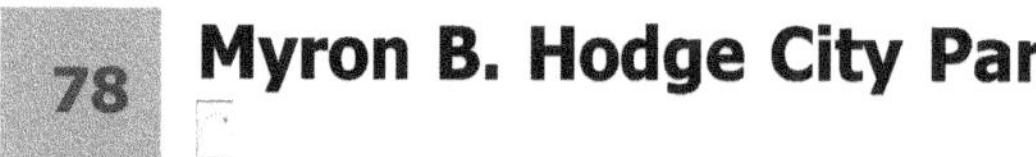

| 78 | **Myron B. Hodge City Park** |

County: Wakulla
Nearest city: Sopchoppy
Physical address: 220 Park Ave., Sopchoppy, 32358

Coordinates: 30.050507° N, -84.498079° W

Gazetteer page: 49 and 50

Size: 50 acres

If you're in the area, it's worth stopping by briefy to visit this small city park on the Sopchoppy River. Check the boardwalk and waterfront for night-herons and Prothonotary Warblers, and hike the short trail to the left side of the property upon entering. In the thicker hardwoods of the hiking trail you'll find migrants like Yellow-billed Cuckoos in spring, as well as Mississippi and Swallow-tailed Kites circling overhead in warmer months. This site can be a busy boat launch in warm weather. Consider launching a canoe from this spot to explore the Sopchoppy River more extensively.

Directions: From the intersection of Rose St. and US 319/SR 377/Sopchoppy Hwy. in Sopchoppy, head south on Sopchoppy Hwy. for 0.4 mi. Turn right (west) on Sheldon St. and go 0.4 mi. Turn left (south) on Park Ave. and drive 0.5 mi. The entrance is on the right (west) side of the road.

Open dawn to dusk. (850) 962-4611, (850) 962-5486
www.sopchoppy.org

Named for its fast, darting fight, the Whirlabout is a common "grass skipper" that occurs in the Panhandle and peninsula most of the year. Host plants for the caterpillar include a variety of grasses. Shepherd's needle and lantana provide nectar for adults.

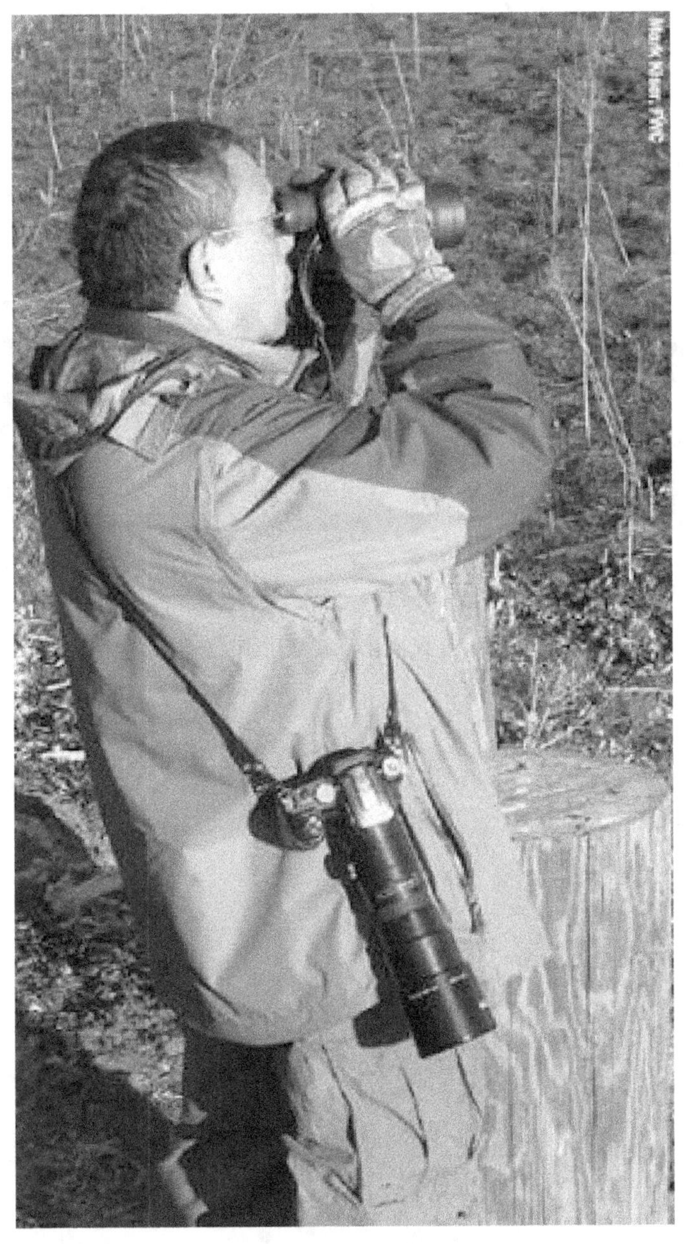

Birders and wildlife watchers contribute nearly $5 billion to Florida's economy each year.

St. Vincent National Wildlife Refuge

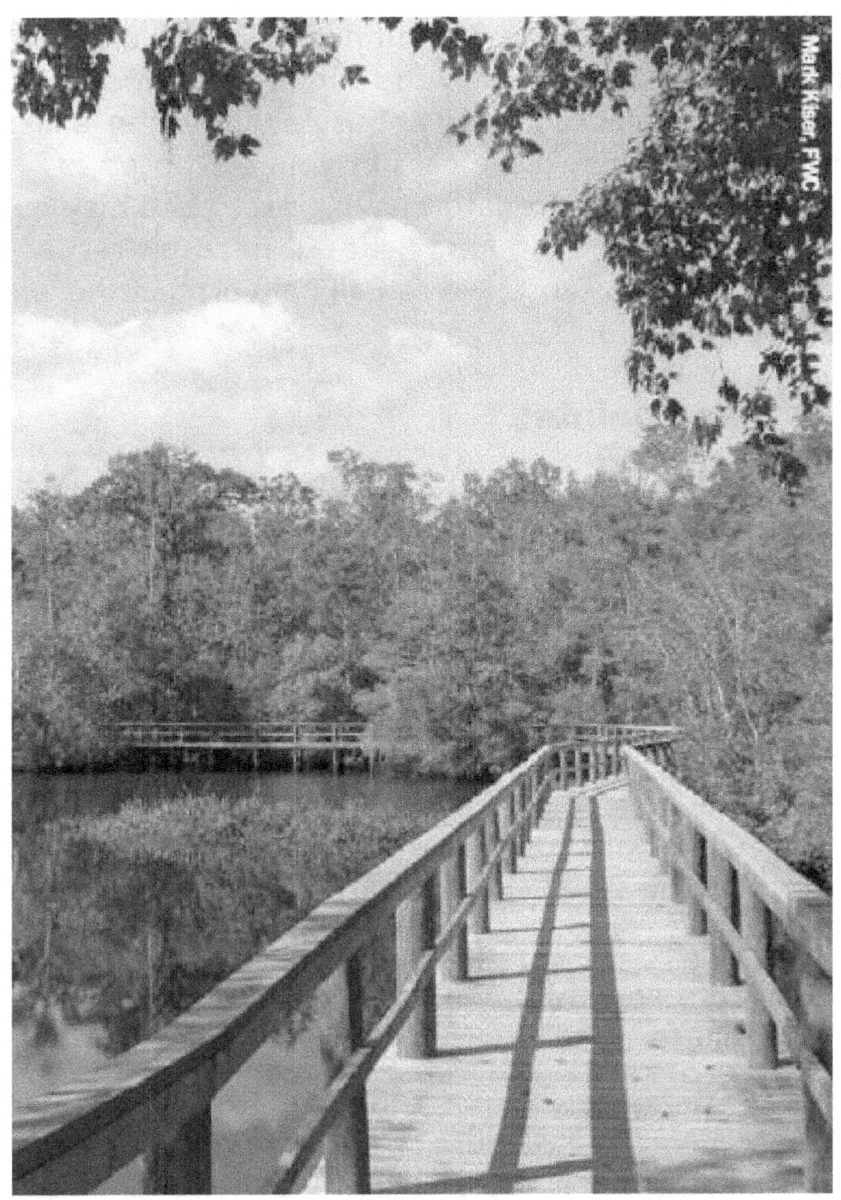

Myron B. Hodge City Park

Birding and wildlife viewing ethics

Don't you hate it when the doorbell or telephone rings just as you settle down to dinner or a nap? While mere nuisances to us, disruptions in feeding and nesting routines can spell disaster for birds and other wildlife, especially the cumulative effect of frequent disruptions, a common occurrence at busy sites. When a nesting bird is forced to fy, it may leave eggs or young exposed to temperature extremes or predators. A migratory bird may be exhausted and hungry from a long fight — it needs to rest and eat. With care and common sense, we can all help protect the wildlife we love to watch.

Consider these points:

- Stay back from concentrations of nesting or loafing waterbirds — a spotting scope may be a better choice than binoculars.

- Walk around groups of birds on the beach rather than forcing them to fy.

- Sit or crouch so that you appear smaller. Keep movements slow and steady rather than fast or sporadic.

- If viewing from your car, stay inside as much as possible. It acts as a viewing "blind" and the birds are less likely to fy if they don't recognize you as human.

- Stay on roads, trails and paths to minimize habitat disturbance.

- Do you occasionally use recordings to attract birds? If so, remember not to overuse them, or to try to attract rare or protected species. Also, do not use them during the nesting season. Be aware that some locations prohibit the use of recordings.

- For more information, please see the American Birding Association's Code of Ethics at www.aba.org/about/ethics.html, FWC's viewing ethics at

Birding and wildlife viewing resources

There are many more resources for birding and wildlife viewing in Florida! Before your trip, check the Internet for area rare bird alert hotlines and statewide birding listservs to get an idea of what's being seen. If you're staying in an area for a longer visit, check local book and nature stores for area guides published by local Audubon chapters or birders. The Great Florida Birding and Wildlife Trail guidebooks and the trip-planning tool at foridabirdingtrail.com are just a taste of the information available to plan your ultimate Florida birding and wildlife viewing vacation!

For more information...

Or to be added to the mailing list for the Great Florida Birding and Wildlife Trail's newsletter, *Kite Tales*, write to:

Great Florida Birding and Wildlife Trail (or GFBWT)
620 South Meridian Street
Tallahassee, FL 32399-1600

You may also view *Kite Tales* on the GFBWT website at floridabirdingtrail.com.

The *Kite Tales* newsletter includes news about the Trail and Trail-related events across the state. Information also is available regarding Trail sponsorship, site nominations for upcoming Trail sections, tips for better birding and the economic impact of this fourishing pastime. Take part in the continued development of this great resource for birders and wildlife watchers of all skill levels, while enjoying and ensuring continued concern for the conservation of Florida's fabulous avian and wildlife treasures!

Birders and wildlife viewers! Flex your economic muscles!

Florida communities have long made land use choices to attract traditional tourists and their dollars. Birding and wildlife viewing are big business in Florida too, but communities will only recognize that if we're visible! Your visibility and economic impact can encourage wildlife conservation.

Some ways you can make yourself more visible:

- Wear bird and wildlife t-shirts.

- Take your binoculars into the restaurant with you.

- Ask local residents in restaurants, hotels, gas stations etc. about where good birding and wildlife viewing locations might be in their area.

- Leave birder calling cards whenever you spend money, helping vendors make the connection between healthy wildlands and healthy economies (cards may be downloaded from www.foridabirdingtrail.com).

- Put a birding bumper sticker or window decal on your car or business. It speaks for itself, so you don't have to!

Conserve wildlife by watching wildlife! It's more than a hobby... it's a legacy.

For the birds!

The Great Florida Birding and Wildlife Trail helps everyone enjoy and conserve Florida's wildlife and wildlife habitat. A donation to the Wildlife Foundation of Florida helps us expand and enhance the Birding and Wildlife Trail experience. With your support, we can continue to protect Florida's natural resources for future generations to enjoy.

If you would like to make a donation, please mail your check to:

Wildlife Foundation of Florida
Attn: GFBWT
P.O. Box 6181
Tallahassee, FL 32314-6181

Note: Please write GFBWT in the memo section of your check!

You may also make a donation via credit card at
wildlifefoundationofflorida.com/birding

What's new?
Follow us on Facebook and Twitter at MyGFBT.

View our blog at
onthetrailfwc.wordpress.com

Support Conservation and the Birding and Wildlife Trail!

Book a Room! Reserve a hotel room, anywhere in the world, at an InterContinental Hotel (including Holiday Inn, Crowne Plaza and Candlewood Suites) and 5% of your stay will be donated to the

Wildlife Foundation of Florida. To "give back" to conservation, all reservations must be made through our affiliate's link at wildlifefoundationofflorida.com/birding.

Order Your Official GFBWT Merchandise! We offer several T-shirt designs, stylish baseball caps, binoculars, patches, stickers, flash drives and more. Proudly wearing birding apparel and displaying birding stickers on your vehicle help communities recognize you as a wildlife watcher and conservationist, and sale proceeds benefit the Birding and Wildlife Trail program. Order yours today at floridabirdingtrail.com and wildlifefoundationofflorida.com/birding!

Sharing Florida's public lands during hunting season

Florida's residents and visitors are fortunate to have an abundance of public and private lands open for wildlife viewing and other outdoor recreation. Seasonal hunting takes place on many of these public lands that are part of the Great Florida Birding and Wildlife Trail. Some of these lands - wildlife management areas and wildlife refuges – were acquired and are managed with revenue generated from the sale of hunting licenses and taxes on various types of sporting goods. Birders and hunters can and do share these lands, as well as a love for the outdoors and conservation.

Some Birding and Wildlife Trail sites are closed during hunting seasons. Other sites allow multiple activities, including birding and hiking, to take place during hunts. If the site you plan to visit has a hunting icon in this guidebook, please visit the FWC's website at MyFWC.com/hunting or MyFWC.com/viewing/recreation to find information on hunting seasons, dates, times of day, area closures, regulations, WMA maps and more. In the words of Pete Dunne, legendary birder, author (and hunter, too), "awareness of your state's (and site's) hunting regulations, and what game is, and is not, in season, will help you make better decisions in the field." Trip planning is important – do your homework prior to arriving at your destination. Birders need not stay home, nor avoid all huntable lands, during hunting season. However, when venturing outdoors during hunting season, wear blaze orange for visibility and safety.

Birders and hunters in Florida have access to one of the largest wildlife management area (WMA) systems in the United States, with nearly 6 million acres of lands established as WMAs or Wildlife and Environmental Areas (WEAs). On the majority of these lands, the FWC is a cooperating manager working in conjunction with other government agencies and private landowners to conserve wildlife and provide quality outdoor experiences for the public. The FWC is the landowner or "lead" managing agency for nearly 50 WMAs and WEAs totaling millions of acres. On these lands, the FWC is responsible for land stewardship, wildlife conservation and a wide range of recreation activities including birding, hunting, fishing and wildlife viewing. The FWC's Office of Public Access and Wildlife Viewing Services, where the Great Florida Birding and Wildlife Trail program is administered, also develops public access amenities on these lead WMAs.